Life in al-Barzakh

Life After Death

Editor Al-eImam Ahmad
Al-Azhar Publications

The Noble Features of the Prophet

(Peace Be Upon Him)

And We have sent you (O Muhammad) not but as a mercy for the 'Alamin (mankind, jinns and all that exists). (21:107)

وَمَآ أَرۡسَلۡنَٰكَ إِلَّا رَحۡمَةٗ لِّلۡعَٰلَمِينَ ١٠٧

The Prophet was neither tall nor was he short. He was of medium stature. In complexion, he was neither very white, nor very dark. His hair was neither very straight nor very curly (but slightly wavy). When he attained the age of forty, Allah the Almighty granted him Prophethood. He lived for ten years in Makkah and in Madina for ten years. At that time there were not more than twenty white hair on his blessed head and beard. The seal of prophethood was situated between his shoulders. He was the last of the Prophets (Peace be Upon Them). He was the most generous and the most truthful. He was the most kind-hearted and came from a most noble family. Any person who saw him suddenly would become awe-inspired. He had such a great personality and dignity, that the person who saw him for the first time, because of his awe-inspiring personality, would be overcome with a feeling of profound respect. Anyone who came in close contact with him, and knew his excellent character was smitten with the love of his excellent attributes. Anyone who described his noble features can only say:

“I have not seen anyone like the Messenger of Allah (peace be upon him) neither before nor after him.”

Ibn Kathir

Ismail Ibn Kathir was born c. 1300, and died 1373. He was a highly influential Sunni scholar of the Shafi'i school during the Mamluk rule of Syria, an expert on tafsir (Quranic exegesis) and faqīh (jurisprudence) as well as a historian.

Other Books by Ibn Kathir and Ibn Al-Qayyim

Stories of the Prophets	ISBN: 9781643543888
Timeless Seeds of Advice	ISBN: 9781643544069
Diseases of the Hearts & Cures	ISBN 9781643544106
The Noble Quran (Arabic)	ISBN: 9781643543994
Koran (English: Easy to Read)	ISBN: 9781643540924
The Path to Guidance	ISBN: 9781643544052
Miracles of the Prophet	ISBN: 9781643544038
Seerah of Prophet Muhammad	ISBN: 9781643543222
Book on Islam and Marriage	ISBN: 9781073877140
Great Women of Islam	ISBN: 9781643543758
Stories of the Koran	ISBN: 9781095900796
The Purification of the Soul	ISBN: 9781643541389
Al-Fawaid: Wise Sayings	ISBN: 9781727812718
The Book of Hajj	ISBN: 9781072243335
40 Hadith Qudsi	ISBN: 9781070655949
40 Hadith Nawawi	ISBN: 9781070547428
The Legacy of the Prophet	ISBN: 9781080249343
The Ideal Muslim Woman	ISBN: 9781643543192
The Soul's Journey after Death	ISBN: 9781643541365
Ota Benga	ISBN: 9781643543802
Don't Be Sad	ISBN: 9781643543451
Khalid Bin Al-Waleed	ISBN: 9781643543420
The Islamic View of Jesus	ISBN: 9781643543352

How can you disbelieve in Allah? Seeing that you were dead and He gave you life. Then He will give you death, then again will bring you to life (on the Day of Resurrection) and then unto Him you will return.

كَيْفَ تَكْفُرُونَ بِٱللَّهِ وَكُنتُمْ أَمْوَٰتًا فَأَحْيَٰكُمْ ۖ ثُمَّ يُمِيتُكُمْ ثُمَّ يُحْيِيكُمْ ثُمَّ إِلَيْهِ تُرْجَعُونَ ﴿٢٨﴾

Indeed, in the creation of the heavens and earth, and the alternation of the night and the day, and the [great] ships which sail through the sea with that which benefits people, and what Allah has sent down from the heavens of rain, giving life thereby to the earth after its lifelessness and dispersing therein every [kind of] moving creature, and [His] directing of the winds and the clouds controlled between the heaven and the earth are signs for a people who use reason.

إِنَّ فِى خَلْقِ ٱلسَّمَٰوَٰتِ وَٱلْأَرْضِ وَٱخْتِلَٰفِ ٱلَّيْلِ وَٱلنَّهَارِ وَٱلْفُلْكِ ٱلَّتِى تَجْرِى فِى ٱلْبَحْرِ بِمَا يَنفَعُ ٱلنَّاسَ وَمَآ أَنزَلَ ٱللَّهُ مِنَ ٱلسَّمَآءِ مِن مَّآءٍ فَأَحْيَا بِهِ ٱلْأَرْضَ بَعْدَ مَوْتِهَا وَبَثَّ فِيهَا مِن كُلِّ دَآبَّةٍ وَتَصْرِيفِ ٱلرِّيَٰحِ وَٱلسَّحَابِ ٱلْمُسَخَّرِ بَيْنَ ٱلسَّمَآءِ وَٱلْأَرْضِ لَءَايَٰتٍ لِّقَوْمٍ يَعْقِلُونَ ﴿١٦٤﴾

Have you not considered those who left their homes in many thousands, fearing death? Allah said to them, "Die"; then He restored them to life. And Allah is full of bounty to the people, but most of the people do not show gratitude.

۞ أَلَمْ تَرَ إِلَى ٱلَّذِينَ خَرَجُوا۟ مِن دِيَٰرِهِمْ وَهُمْ أُلُوفٌ حَذَرَ
ٱلْمَوْتِ فَقَالَ لَهُمُ ٱللَّهُ مُوتُوا۟ ثُمَّ أَحْيَٰهُمْ ۚ إِنَّ ٱللَّهَ لَذُو فَضْلٍ عَلَى
ٱلنَّاسِ وَلَٰكِنَّ أَكْثَرَ ٱلنَّاسِ لَا يَشْكُرُونَ ﴿٢٤٣﴾

Have you not considered the one who argued with Abraham about his Lord [merely] because Allah had given him kingship? When Abraham said, "My Lord is the one who gives life and causes death," he said, "I give life and cause death." Abraham said, "Indeed, Allah brings up the sun from the east, so bring it up from the west." So the disbeliever was overwhelmed [by astonishment], and Allah does not guide the wrongdoing people.

أَلَمْ تَرَ إِلَى ٱلَّذِى حَآجَّ إِبْرَٰهِـۧمَ فِى رَبِّهِۦٓ أَنْ ءَاتَىٰهُ ٱللَّهُ ٱلْمُلْكَ إِذْ
قَالَ إِبْرَٰهِـۧمُ رَبِّىَ ٱلَّذِى يُحْىِۦ وَيُمِيتُ قَالَ أَنَا۠ أُحْىِۦ وَأُمِيتُ ۖ قَالَ
إِبْرَٰهِـۧمُ فَإِنَّ ٱللَّهَ يَأْتِى بِٱلشَّمْسِ مِنَ ٱلْمَشْرِقِ فَأْتِ بِهَا مِنَ ٱلْمَغْرِبِ
فَبُهِتَ ٱلَّذِى كَفَرَ ۗ وَٱللَّهُ لَا يَهْدِى ٱلْقَوْمَ ٱلظَّٰلِمِينَ ﴿٢٥٨﴾

Or [consider such an example] as the one who passed by a township which had fallen into ruin. He said, "How will Allah bring this to life after its death?" So Allah caused him to die for a hundred years; then He revived him. He said, "How long have you remained?" The man said, "I have remained a day or part of a day." He said, "Rather, you have remained one hundred years. Look at your food and your drink; it has not changed with time. And look at your donkey; and We will make you a sign for the people. And look at the bones [of this donkey] - how We raise them and then We cover them with flesh." And when it became clear to him, he said, "I know that Allah is over all things competent."

أَوْ كَٱلَّذِى مَرَّ عَلَىٰ قَرْيَةٍ وَهِىَ خَاوِيَةٌ عَلَىٰ عُرُوشِهَا قَالَ أَنَّىٰ يُحْىِۦ
هَٰذِهِ ٱللَّهُ بَعْدَ مَوْتِهَا ۖ فَأَمَاتَهُ ٱللَّهُ مِا۟ئَةَ عَامٍ ثُمَّ بَعَثَهُۥ ۖ قَالَ كَمْ لَبِثْتَ ۖ
قَالَ لَبِثْتُ يَوْمًا أَوْ بَعْضَ يَوْمٍ ۖ قَالَ بَل لَّبِثْتَ مِا۟ئَةَ عَامٍ فَٱنظُرْ
إِلَىٰ طَعَامِكَ وَشَرَابِكَ لَمْ يَتَسَنَّهْ ۖ وَٱنظُرْ إِلَىٰ حِمَارِكَ
وَلِنَجْعَلَكَ ءَايَةً لِّلنَّاسِ ۖ وَٱنظُرْ إِلَى ٱلْعِظَامِ كَيْفَ
نُنشِزُهَا ثُمَّ نَكْسُوهَا لَحْمًا ۚ فَلَمَّا تَبَيَّنَ لَهُۥ قَالَ أَعْلَمُ أَنَّ ٱللَّهَ
عَلَىٰ كُلِّ شَىْءٍ قَدِيرٌ ﴿٢٥٩﴾

Every soul will taste death, and you will only be given your [full] compensation on the Day of Resurrection. So he who is drawn away from the Fire and admitted to Paradise has attained [his desire]. And what is the life of this world except the enjoyment of delusion.

كُلُّ نَفۡسٖ ذَآئِقَةُ ٱلۡمَوۡتِۗ وَإِنَّمَا تُوَفَّوۡنَ أُجُورَكُمۡ يَوۡمَ
ٱلۡقِيَٰمَةِۖ فَمَن زُحۡزِحَ عَنِ ٱلنَّارِ وَأُدۡخِلَ ٱلۡجَنَّةَ فَقَدۡ فَازَۗ وَمَا
ٱلۡحَيَوٰةُ ٱلدُّنۡيَآ إِلَّا مَتَٰعُ ٱلۡغُرُورِ ١٨٥

Say, "Indeed, my prayer, my rites of sacrifice, my living and my dying are for Allah , Lord of the worlds.

قُلۡ إِنَّ صَلَاتِي وَنُسُكِي وَمَحۡيَايَ وَمَمَاتِي لِلَّهِ رَبِّ ٱلۡعَٰلَمِينَ ١٦٢

Say, [O Muhammad], "O mankind, indeed I am the Messenger of Allah to you all, [from Him] to whom belongs the dominion of the heavens and the earth. There is no deity except Him; He gives life and causes death." So believe in Allah and His Messenger, the unlettered prophet, who believes in Allah and His words, and follow him that you may be guided.

قُلْ يَٰٓأَيُّهَا ٱلنَّاسُ إِنِّى رَسُولُ ٱللَّهِ إِلَيْكُمْ جَمِيعًا ٱلَّذِى لَهُۥ
مُلْكُ ٱلسَّمَٰوَٰتِ وَٱلْأَرْضِ ۖ لَآ إِلَٰهَ إِلَّا هُوَ يُحْىِۦ وَيُمِيتُ ۖ فَـَٔامِنُوا۟
بِٱللَّهِ وَرَسُولِهِ ٱلنَّبِىِّ ٱلْأُمِّىِّ ٱلَّذِى يُؤْمِنُ بِٱللَّهِ وَكَلِمَٰتِهِۦ
وَٱتَّبِعُوهُ لَعَلَّكُمْ تَهْتَدُونَ ﴿١٥٨﴾

Indeed, to Allah belongs the dominion of the heavens and the earth; He gives life and causes death. And you have not besides Allah any protector or any helper.

إِنَّ ٱللَّهَ لَهُۥ مُلْكُ ٱلسَّمَٰوَٰتِ وَٱلْأَرْضِ ۖ يُحْىِۦ وَيُمِيتُ ۚ وَمَا لَكُم مِّن
دُونِ ٱللَّهِ مِن وَلِىٍّ وَلَا نَصِيرٍ ﴿١١٦﴾

He gives life and causes death, and to Him you will be returned

هُوَ يُحْيِۦ وَيُمِيتُ وَإِلَيْهِ تُرْجَعُونَ ﴿٥٦﴾

And indeed, it is We who give life and cause death, and We are the Inheritor.

وَإِنَّا لَنَحْنُ نُحْيِۦ وَنُمِيتُ وَنَحْنُ ٱلْوَٰرِثُونَ ﴿٢٣﴾

And Allah sends down rain from the skies, and gives therewith life to the earth after its death: verily in this is a Sign for those who listen.

وَٱللَّهُ أَنزَلَ مِنَ ٱلسَّمَآءِ مَآءً فَأَحْيَا بِهِ ٱلْأَرْضَ بَعْدَ مَوْتِهَآ ۚ إِنَّ فِي ذَٰلِكَ لَءَايَةً
لِّقَوْمٍ يَسْمَعُونَ ﴿٦٥﴾

Then [if you had], We would have made you taste double [punishment in] life and double [after] death. Then you would not find for yourself against Us a helper.

إِذًا لَّأَذَقْنَٰكَ ضِعْفَ ٱلْحَيَوٰةِ وَضِعْفَ ٱلْمَمَاتِ ثُمَّ لَا تَجِدُ لَكَ
عَلَيْنَا نَصِيرًا ﴿٧٥﴾

And it is He who gives life and causes death, and His is the alternation of the night and the day. Then will you not reason?

وَهُوَ ٱلَّذِى يُحْىِۦ وَيُمِيتُ وَلَهُ ٱخْتِلَٰفُ ٱلَّيْلِ وَٱلنَّهَارِ ۚ أَفَلَا
تَعْقِلُونَ ﴿٨٠﴾

(In Falsehood will they be) Until, when death comes to one of them, he says: "O my Lord! send me back (to life),-

حَتَّىٰٓ إِذَا جَآءَ أَحَدَهُمُ ٱلْمَوْتُ قَالَ رَبِّ ٱرْجِعُونِ ﴿٩٩﴾

But they have taken besides Him gods which create nothing, while they are created, and possess not for themselves any harm or benefit and possess not [power to cause] death or life or resurrection.

وَٱتَّخَذُوا۟ مِن دُونِهِۦٓ ءَالِهَةً لَّا يَخْلُقُونَ شَيْـًٔا وَهُمْ يُخْلَقُونَ وَلَا
يَمْلِكُونَ لِأَنفُسِهِمْ ضَرًّا وَلَا نَفْعًا وَلَا يَمْلِكُونَ مَوْتًا وَلَا حَيَوٰةً وَلَا
نُشُورًا ﴿٣﴾

CHAPTER 1

THE APPROACH OF DEATH

Loving to Meet Allāh

A true believer's greatest wish and ultimate hope is to meet his Lord (🏵) and be able to see Him in the hereafter. 'Ubādah Bin aṣ-Ṣamit (🏵) reported that the Prophet (🏵) said:

> ‹Whoever loves to meet Allāh, Allāh loves to meet him; and whoever hates to meet Allāh, Allāh hates to meet him.›

On hearing this, 'Ā'ishah (🏵) exclaimed, "But we do hate death!" The Prophet (🏵) responded:

> ‹This is not what it means! When death comes to a believer, he is given the tidings of Allāh's acceptance and bounties. Nothing is then dearer to him than what is ahead: he loves to meet Allāh; and Allāh loves to meet him. But when death comes to a disbeliever, he is given the tidings of Allāh's torture and punishment. Nothing is then more hateful to him than what is ahead: he hates to meet Allāh; and Allāh hates to meet him.› [1]

Similar to this is Abū Hurayrah's *ḥadīth* (presented in full in Chapter 2) that Allāh's Messenger (🏵) said:

> ‹Verily, when death descends upon a believer, and he witnesses things (implying his forthcoming rewards),

---

1 Al-Bukhārī and Muslim.

he wishes that his soul would depart (quickly), and Allāh loves to meet him ...

And when death descends upon an enemy of Allāh, and he witnesses things (implying his imminent punishment), he wishes that his soul would never depart, and Allāh hates to meet him.› [1]

Allāh Hesitates to Take a Believer's Soul

Allāh (ﷻ) loves the believers in proportion to their obedience to Him and His Messenger (ﷺ). When Allāh loves a person, he becomes so supportive to him and so protective that He would prevent any harm from reaching him, and He would even hesitate to inflict death on him – except that it is an avoidable thing that He (ﷻ) had decreed for all human beings. Abū Hurayrah (رضي الله عنه) reported that Allāh's Messenger (ﷺ) said that Allāh (ﷻ) said:

‹Whoever harms a *walī* [2] **of Mine, I declare war against him.**

My *'abd* [3] **does not draw closer to Me with anything dearer to Me than the religious duties I have mandated upon him.**

And My *'abd* continues to draw closer to Me with voluntary acts (of worship) until I love him; when I love him, I become his ears with which he hears, his eyes with which he sees, his hand with which he strikes and his foot with which he walks. Would he then ask me for anything, I surely grant it to him; and would he seek refuge in Me, I surely shelter him.

1 Recorded by al-Bazzār; verified to be authentic by al-Albānī (*aṣ-Ṣaḥīḥah* no. 2628).

2 *Walī*: Ally.

3 *'Abd*: A slave or worshipper.

I do not hesitate in anything I have to do as I hesitate in taking the life of my believing *'abd*: he hates death and I hate to hurt him.› [1]

Satan's Presence at the Time of Death

Shayṭān [2] works hard to entice people to commit evil actions. He is intent to be present when a person does any action that he may be able to influence by introducing into it any possible amount of sinning. The moment of death is a final chance that *Shayṭān* wants to try, hoping to make the dying person end his life with evil, impiety, or disobedience. Jābir Bin 'Abdillāh (رضي الله عنه) reported that the Prophet (ﷺ) said:

‹Verily the *Shayṭān* attends with you in all your actions. He attends when you eat; if any morsel of food drops, wipe the dirt off it, and eat it instead of leaving it for the *Shayṭān*. After finishing, lick your fingers, because you do not know where in the food the blessing lies.› [3]

The Disbeliever's Wish to Return to Life

As indicated in the *ḥadīth*s of 'Ubādah and Abū Hurayrah (رضي الله عنهما) (p. 1 above), when the reality of death comes to a believer, he welcomes it and longs to meet his Lord (عز وجل). A disbeliever, on the other hand, fears such a meeting and hates it. Allāh (تعالى) says:

﴿حَتَّىٰٓ إِذَا جَآءَ أَحَدَهُمُ ٱلْمَوْتُ قَالَ رَبِّ ٱرْجِعُونِ ۝ لَعَلِّيٓ
أَعْمَلُ صَٰلِحًا فِيمَا تَرَكْتُ كَلَّآ إِنَّهَا كَلِمَةٌ هُوَ قَآئِلُهَا وَمِن

1 Al-Bukhārī.

2 *Shayṭān*: Satan.

3 Muslim.

وَرَآئِهِم بَرْزَخٌ إِلَىٰ يَوْمِ يُبْعَثُونَ ۞ ﴾ المؤمنون ٩٩−١٠٠

«Until, when death comes to one of them (those who join partners with Allāh), he says, "My Lord! Send me back. Perhaps I may do good in that which I have left behind!" No! It is but a word that he speaks, and behind them is a barrier until the day when they are raised up.» [1]

Agonies of Death

Death arrives with pains and agonies of which no human being is spared – not even the prophets. 'Ā'ishah (🙏) reported that Allāh's Messenger (ﷺ) said:

‹Lā ilāha illallāh [2]. Verily death comes with agonies.› [3]

Too Late for the Disbelievers to Declare Faith

A disbeliever's declaration of faith at the time of Death will be rejected. Ibn 'Abbās (🙏) reported that Allāh's Messenger (ﷺ) said:

‹When Allāh (ﷻ) drowned Pharaoh, he said, "(Now) I believe that there is no (true) god except Him in Whom the children of Israel believe." Jibrīl said, "O Muḥammad, would you have seen me as I took black dirt from the sea and stuffed it into his mouth, fearing that the Mercy might reach him."› [4]

---

1   *Al-Mu'minūn* 23:99-100.
2   There is no deity worthy of worship but Allāh.
3   Al-Bukhārī and Aḥmad.
4   Recorded by Aḥmad and at-Tirmithī; verified to be authentic by al-Albānī (*Ṣaḥīḥ ul-Jāmi'* no. 5206).

The First Step into the Hereafter

Death is the first step into the hereafter, and the grave is the first of the hereafter's domiciles. Hānī, 'Uthmān Bin 'Affān's (⁕) servant, said that whenever 'Uthmān stood over a grave, he would cry until he soaked his beard. He was told, "You remember *Jannah* and the Fire without weeping, but you weep when you remember the grave!" He replied, "Indeed, I heard Allāh's Messenger (⁕) say:

> ‹The grave is the first of the hereafter's domiciles; if one passes through it safely, what follows will be easier; and if one does not pass through it safely, what follows will be more horrible.›

And I heard Allāh's Messenger (⁕) say:

> ‹I have never seen a dreadful view but the grave is even more dreadful.› " [1]

---

1 Recorded by at-Tirmithī; verified to be authentic by al-Albānī (*Saḥīḥ ut-Targhībi wat-Tarhīb*).

CHAPTER 2

TEXTS DESCRIBING *AL-BARZAKH*

In this chapter, we present a number of long *ḥadīth*s, each describing various happenings in *al-Barzakh*. The incidents mentioned in these (as well as other *ḥadīth*s) are summarized and segmented in the next four chapters to cover the four stages of the life of *al-Barzakh*.

1. Al-Barā''s *Ḥadīth*

Al-Barā' Bin 'Āzib (ﷺ) reported that they (the companions) went out with Allāh's Messenger (ﷺ) to the funeral of a man from *al-Anṣār* [1]. They reached the location of the grave before it was dug. The Messenger (ﷺ) sat down facing the *Qiblah* [2]; and they sat around him quietly, as if afraid to disturb birds standing on their heads. He held in his hand a stick with which he was moving the earth. He looked toward the sky, then toward the earth, raising and lowering his eyes three times. He said to them (two or three times), ‹**Seek refuge in Allāh (ﷻ) from the punishment of the grave.**› Then he said (three times):

> ‹**O Allāh, I seek refuge in You from the punishment of the grave.**›

He (ﷺ) continued:

> ‹**Verily, when a believing *'abd* [3] is at the point of departure from the worldly life, and is about to**

1 These are the companions of the Prophet (ﷺ) from al-Madīnah who helped and supported him when he migrated to them.

2 The *Qiblah*: The direction of *al-Ka'bah*.

3 A slave, servant, or created being of Allāh (ﷻ).

enter the next life [1], angels descend from heaven. Their faces are white (and bright) like the sun. They carry with them a shroud from the clothes of *Jannah*, and embalmment from the fragrance of *Jannah*. They sit away from him at the limit of his eyesight. The angel of death then arrives, sits by his head, and says, "O good and peaceful soul, depart to Allāh's forgiveness and pleasure." On hearing this, the soul leaves the body (as easily) as water drops flow from the spout of a water skin; and he (the Angel of Death) takes it.

When the soul leaves his body, all angels between the heavens and the earth, and all angels in the heavens, pronounce *ṣalāh* on him [2]. All gates of the heavens open for him; the guardians of every gate implore Allāh that this soul ascends in their direction.

When the Angel of Death takes the soul, they (the other angels) do not leave it in his hand for as little as the blinking of an eye. They take it and place it in their shroud and embalmment. To this apply Allāh's (ﷻ) words:

﴿تَوَفَّتْهُ رُسُلُنَا وَهُمْ لاَ يُفَرِّطُونَ ۝﴾ الأنعام ٦١

«...Our messengers (the angels) take his soul, and they never neglect their duty.» [3]

There emanates then from the soul the best smelling scent of musk that ever existed on the surface of the earth.

The angels then ascend with it. As they pass by gatherings of angels, they ask them, "What is this good soul?" They (the angels holding it) reply, "He

1 **i.e., he is close to death.**

2 i.e. they ask that he be forgiven.

3 *Al-An'ām* 6:61.

is so and so, son of so and so," using the best names with which he had been addressed in the first life. When they reach the lowest heaven, they ask for permission to enter; and the gates open for them. The most elite (angels) of each heaven escort him to the next one, until he reaches the seventh heaven. Allāh (ﷻ) then says, "Write My servant's records in *'Illiyyūn* [1],

﴿وَمَا أَدْرَاكَ مَا عِلِّيُّونَ ۝﴾ المطففين ١٩

«And what will make you know what *'Illiyyūn* is? An inscribed register, witnessed by those nearest (to Allāh – among the angels).» [2]"

Thus, his records are inscribed in *'Illiyyūn*; and the angels are told, "Take him back to the earth, because I promised them that from it I create them, into it I return them, and from it I resurrect them once again. [3]"

He is then returned to the earth; and his soul is returned to his body, so that he hears the thumping of his companions' shoes as they walk away from his grave.

Two angels of severe reprimand then come to him, and shake him. They make him sit up, and ask him, "Who is you Lord?" He replies, "My Lord is Allāh." They ask him, "What is your *Dīn* (religion)?" He replies, "My *Dīn* is *Islām*." They ask him, "Who is that man who was sent to you?" He replies, "He is Allāh's Messenger (ﷺ)." They ask him, "What did you do?" He replies, "I read Allāh's Book, believed in it, and obeyed it." They shake him again, asking,

1 A place most high; the highest register.

2 *Al-Muṭaffifīn* 83:19-21.

3 *Ṭāhā* 20:55.

"Who is your Lord? What is your *Dīn*? Who is your Prophet?" And this is the last *fitnah* (trial) to which a believer is subjected. In this regard, Allāh (ﷻ) says:

﴿يُثَبِّتُ ٱللَّهُ ٱلَّذِينَ ءَامَنُواْ بِٱلْقَوْلِ ٱلثَّابِتِ فِي ٱلْحَيَوٰةِ ٱلدُّنْيَا وَفِي ٱلْآخِرَةِ﴾ إبراهيم ٢٧

«Allāh keeps the believers firm with firm words in the first life, and in the last one.» [1]

He repeats, "My Lord is Allāh, my *Dīn* is *Islām*, and my Prophet is Muḥammad (ﷺ)." A caller then calls from the heavens, "My servant has spoken the truth; so provide him with furnishings from *Jannah*; clothe him from *Jannah*; and open for him a door to *Jannah*." Thus he receives provision and perfume from it; and his grave is spread to the extent of his eyesight.

Before him appears a man with a pleasant face, nice garments, and a good smell. He says to him, "I am to give you glad tidings that will please you: tidings of Allāh's acceptance, and gardens with everlasting bliss. This is the day that you have been promised." He responds, "Glad tidings from Allāh be to you too. Who are you? Your face is one that brings goodness." He says, "I am your good deeds. By Allāh, I only knew you quick in obeying Allāh, and slow in disobeying Him. May Allāh reward you with good."

A door is opened for him to *Jannah* and another one to the Fire; and he is told, "This (the Fire) would have been your dwelling had you disobeyed Allāh. But Allāh has substituted it for you with this (*Jannah*)." When he sees what is awaiting him in

1 *Ibrāhīm* 14:27.

Jannah (of pleasures), he says, "O my Lord, speed up the arrival of the Hour (of Resurrection), so that I may rejoin my family and property." He is told, "Calm down."

And verily when a disbelieving (or disobedient) *'abd* is at the point of departure from the worldly life, and is about to enter the hereafter, strong hulking angels with dark faces descend to him from the heavens. They bring with them tough fabrics from the Fire. They sit away from him at the limit of his eyesight. The Angel of Death (عَلَيْهِ السَّلاَمُ) arrives, sits by his head, and says, "O malicious soul, depart to a wrath and anger from Allāh." (On hearing this) it becomes terrified, and clings to the body; but he extracts it (by force), like a skewer is pulled from wet wool, causing the veins and nerves to burst.

Every angel between the heavens and the earth, and every angel in the heavens, curses him. The gates of the heavens are shut; the guardians of every gate implore Allāh that this soul does not ascend in their direction.

When the Angel of Death takes the soul, they (the other angels) do not leave it in his hand for as little as the blinking of an eye. They put it in the fabric that they have (from the Fire); and from it emanates the most repugnant odor of a decaying cadaver that ever existed on the surface of the earth.

The angels then ascend with it. As they pass by gatherings of angels, they ask them, "What is this malicious soul?" The angels holding it respond, "He is so and so, son of so and so," using the worst names with which he had been addressed in the first life. When they reach the lowest heaven, they ask for permission to enter; but the gates are not opened for him. (Here the Messenger (ﷺ) recited:)

﴿لَا تُفَتَّحُ لَهُمْ أَبْوَٰبُ ٱلسَّمَآءِ وَلَا يَدْخُلُونَ ٱلْجَنَّةَ حَتَّىٰ يَلِجَ ٱلْجَمَلُ فِي سَمِّ ٱلْخِيَاطِ﴾ الأعراف ٤٠

«For them (the disbelievers), the gates of heaven will not be opened; and they will not enter *Jannah* until the camel goes through the eye of the needle.» [1]

Allāh (ﷻ) then says, "Write his record in *Sijjīn* [2] in the lowest earth." And they are told, "Take him back to the earth, because I promised them that from it I create them, into it I return them, and from it I resurrect them once again. [3]" His soul is then cast down from the heavens without regard; and it falls into his body. (Here Allāh's Messenger (ﷺ) recited:)

﴿وَمَن يُشْرِكْ بِٱللَّهِ فَكَأَنَّمَا خَرَّ مِنَ ٱلسَّمَآءِ فَتَخْطَفُهُ ٱلطَّيْرُ أَوْ تَهْوِي بِهِ ٱلرِّيحُ فِي مَكَانٍ سَحِيقٍ۝﴾ الحج ٣١

«As for the one who joins partners with Allāh, it is as if he plunges down from the skies – whereupon birds snatch him off, or the wind casts him away to a remote place (from Allāh's mercy).» [4]

His soul is restored to his body, so that he hears the thumping of his companions' shoes as they walk away from his grave.

Two angels of severe reprimand come to him and shake him. They make him sit up, and ask him, "Who is your Lord?" He replies, "Alas, alas, I do not know!" They ask him, "What is your *Dīn*?" He replies, "Alas, alas, I do not know!" They ask him,

1 *Al-A'rāf* 7:40.
2 A place most low; a place of Imprisonment.
3 *Ṭāhā* 20:55.
4 *Al-Ḥajj* 22:31

"Who is that man who was sent to you?" He cannot recall his name, and he is told, "(His name is) Muḥammad!" He says, "Alas, alas, I do not know. I just heard the people say that." He is then told, "You did not know; and you did not recite (the *Qur'ān*)!" A caller calls from the heaven, "He lies! So spread for him furnishings from the Fire; and open for him a door to the Fire." Thus its heat and fierce hot wind reach him; and his grave is tightened around him, causing his ribs to break.

Before him appears a man with ugly face, repulsive clothes, and a foul smell; he says, "I am to give you evil tidings that will displease you. This is the day that you have been promised." He responds, "Evil tidings from Allāh be to you too! Who are you? Your face is one that brings evil." He says, "I am your malicious deeds. By Allāh, I only knew you slow in obeying Allāh, and quick in disobeying Him. May Allāh repay you with evil."

A blind, deaf, and dumb person is appointed for him. He carries in his hand a sledgehammer that, if it hits a mountain, would turn it to dust. He hits him (with it) once; and he becomes dust. Allāh then restores him as he was; and the person hits him again; he sounds a shriek that is heard by everything except men and *jinns*.

A door is opened for him to the Fire; and he is given the furnishings from the Fire. He then says, "O my Lord! Do not establish the Hour."› [1]

1 Recorded by Aḥmad, Abū Dāwūd and others; verified to be authentic by al-Albānī (*Ṣaḥīḥ ul-Jāmi'* no. 1676).

2. Abū Hurayrah's First *Ḥadīth*

Abū Hurayrah (ﷺ) reported that Allāh's Messenger (ﷺ) said:

> **‹Indeed, a dying person is witnessed by angels. If he were righteous, he (the Angel of Death) says, "Depart, O good soul that inhabited a good body; depart in a praised state; and receive glad tidings of happiness, sweet aromas, and a Lord who is not angry." He continues to say this until it leaves the body. It is then taken up to the (first) heaven, where permission is sought for it to be admitted. It is said, "Who is this?" He (an angel) replies, "So and so." It is then said, "Welcome, good soul that inhabited a good body; enter in a praised state; and receive glad tidings of happiness, sweet aromas, and a Lord who is not angry." This repeats (in every heaven), until it finally reaches the (seventh) heaven above which is Allāh (ﷻ).**
>
> **As for an evil man, he (the Angel of Death) says, "Depart, O malicious soul that inhabited a malicious body; depart in a condemned state; and receive evil tidings of boiling fluids and dirty wound discharges (to drink), and other types of suffering of similar nature – all paired together." This continues to be said until it leaves the body. It is then taken up to the (first) heaven, where permission is sought for it to be admitted. It is said, "Who is this?" He (an angel) replies, "So and so." It is then said, "Unwelcome, malicious soul that inhabited a malicious body; return in a condemned state, because the gates to the heavens will not open for you." Thus it is sent down from the heaven, and it enters the grave.**
>
> **The pious person sits in his grave without fear or terror. He is asked, "What did you do?" He replies, "I adhered to *Islām*." He is then asked, "Who is that man?" He replies: "Muhammad, Allāh's**

Messenger (ﷺ). He brought to us clear signs from Allāh; and we believed him." He is then asked, "Did you see Allāh?" He replies, "It is not possible for anyone to see Allāh (in the first life)."

An opening is made (from his grave) to the Fire, so that he sees its various sections crushing each other. He is told, "Look at that from which Allāh (ﷻ) has saved you." Another opening is then made (from his grave) in the direction of *Jannah*; and he views its grandeur and the things (bounties) in it. He is then told, "This will be your position. You lived with certitude (about Allāh's promises); upon it you died; and upon it you will be raised – when Allāh (ﷻ) wills."

The evil person is made to sit in his grave in a state of fear and terror. He is asked, "What did you do?" He replies, "I do not know." He is asked, "Who is that man?" He replies, "I heard the people say things; and I said the same."

An opening then appears (from his grave) in the direction of *Jannah*; and he views its grandeur and the things (bounties) in it. He is told, "Look at that from which Allāh (ﷻ) has deprived you." Another opening appears (from his grave) to the Fire; and he observes its various sections crushing each other. He is told, "This will be your abode; in doubt you lived; upon it you died; and upon it you will be raised – when Allāh wills."› [1]

3. ʿĀʾishah's *Ḥadīth*

ʿĀʾishah (رضي الله عنها) narrated that a Jewish woman came to her door begging for food and saying, "Feed me; may Allāh protect you from the *fitnah*

1 Recorded by Ibn Mājah; verified to be authentic by al-Albānī (*Ṣaḥīḥ ul-Jāmiʿ* no. 1968).

(tribulation) of the *Dajjāl* [1] and the *fitnah* of the grave's torture." 'Ā'ishah (ﷺ) deliberately delayed the woman until Allāh's Messenger (ﷺ) arrived. Then she said, 'O Messenger of Allāh, what does this Jewish woman mean?" He said: **‹What did she say?›** She replied, "She said, 'Feed me; may Allāh protect you from the *fitnah* of the *Dajjāl* and that of the grave's torture.'" Immediately Allāh's Messenger (ﷺ) stood up, raised and extended his hands, and asked Allāh to shelter him from the *fitnah* of the *Dajjāl* and that of the grave's torture. Then he (ﷺ) said:

> **‹As for the *fitnah* of the *Dajjāl*, there never was a prophet but has warned his people from him. However, I will tell you a thing (about the *Dajjāl*) from which no other prophet warned his nation: He is one-eyed; and Allāh is not one-eyed. Between his eyes is written the word "*kāfir*", which every believer will be able to read.**
>
> **And as for the tribulation of the grave: with me will people be tested, and about me will they be asked.**
>
> **A righteous person is made to sit in his grave, without having any fear or terror. He is asked, "What did you use to say about *Islām*?" He is also asked, "Who is that man who was among you?" He replies, "He is Muḥammad, the Messenger of Allāh, who came with clear signs from Allāh; and we believed in him."**
>
> **An opening then appears (from his grave) to the Fire; he observes its various sections crushing each other. He is told, "Look at that from which Allāh (ﷻ) has saved you." Another opening then appears (from his grave) to *Jannah*. He observes its grandeur and the things (bounties) in it. He is told, "This will be your place in it." And he is told, "You lived with certitude (about Allāh); upon that you**

1 The *Dajjāl*: The lying imposter who will claim that he is the Messiah Jesus Son of Mary.

died; and upon it you will be raised – when Allāh wills."

As for an evil person, he is made to sit in his grave in a state of fear and terror. He is asked, "What did you use to say?" He replies, "I heard the people say things; so I said as they said."

An opening then appears (from his grave) to *Jannah*. He observes its grandeur and the things (bounties) in it. He is told, "Look at that from which Allāh has deprived you." Another opening appears (from his grave) to the Fire. He observes its various sections crushing each other. He is told, "This will be your abode in it. You lived in doubt (about Allāh); upon that you died; and upon it will you be raised – when Allāh wills." He is then tortured.› [1]

4. Abū Hurayrah's Second *Ḥadīth*

Abū Hurayrah (⚅) reported that Allāh's Messenger (⚅) said:

‹When a believer dies, the angels of mercy come to him with a piece of white silk. They say, "Depart (from the body) to Allāh's (granted) happiness." It departs with the most beautiful scent of musk. They even pass it from one angel to the next, smelling it.

When they arrive at the gate of the (lowest) heaven, they are asked, "What is this beautiful scent coming from the earth?" They continue their ascent; and as they arrive at each one of the heavens, the same thing is said to them.

They (the angels) take it to (the location of) the souls of the believers. They (the other souls) are happier in meeting it than are those to whom a

---

1   Recorded by Aḥmad; verified to be authentic by al-Albānī in *Ṣaḥīḥ ut-Targhībi wat-Tarhīb*.

beloved one returns after a long absence. They ask it, "What happened to such and such (a disbeliever)?" Some of them interrupt, "Leave him until he rests, because he was in the grief of the world." However, he says, "He died; did he not come to you?" They (the angels) then say, "He was taken to a bottomless pit (of Fire)."

As for a disbeliever, the angels of punishment come to him with coarse fabric and say, "Depart (from the body) to Allāh's wrath." It departs, smelling like the worst of decayed corpses. It is then taken to the gate of the earth.› [1]

5. Abū Hurayrah's Third *Ḥadīth*

Abū Hurayrah (⌀) reported that Allāh's Messenger (⌀) said:

‹When a (believing) dead person is buried, two black and blue angels come to him. One of them is called Munkar, and the other Nakīr. They ask him, "What did you use to say about this man (Muḥammad)?" He says, as he used to say, "He is Allāh's 'abd and Messenger; I testify that there is no deity (worthy of being worshipped) but Allāh, and that Muḥammad is His 'abd and Messenger." They say, "We expected you to say this." His grave is then expanded for him to seventy cubits by seventy; it is illuminated for him; and he is told, "Go to sleep." He says, "Let me return to my people to inform them (about my good condition)." But they tell him, "Sleep as does a newlywed person, whom no one awakens except the member of his family who is dearest to him." (He sleeps like that) until Allāh raises him from his resting place.

[1] Recorded by Ibn Ḥibbān and Ibn Mājah; verified to be authentic by al-Albānī (*Ṣaḥīḥ ut-Targhībi wat-Tarhīb*).

As for a hypocrite, he replies (to their questioning), "I heard the people say things; and I said the same; but I do not know." They say, "We expected you to say this." The earth is then told, "Contract on him." And it contracts on him until his ribs break. Thus, his punishment continues therein, until Allāh raises him from his abode.› [1]

6. Abū Hurayrah's Fourth *Ḥadīth*

Abū Hurayrah (ﷺ) reported that Allāh's Messenger (ﷺ) said:

‹Verily, when death descends upon a believer, and he witnesses things (implying his forthcoming rewards), he wishes that his soul would depart (quickly), and Allāh loves to meet him.

His soul is taken up to the heaven. The souls of the believers come to him and inquire from him about their acquaintances of the dwellers of the earth. They are pleased when he says, "I left such and such in the *dunyā* (the first life)." And when he says, "Such and such had died," they say (disappointedly), "But he was not brought to us." [2]

A believer is made to sit in his grave, and is asked, "Who is your lord?" He replies, "My lord is Allāh." He is asked, "Who is your prophet?" He replies, "My prophet is Muḥammad (ﷺ)." He is asked, "What is your religion?" He says, "My religion is *Islām*." A door is then opened from his grave (to *Jannah*), and he is told, "Look at you

1 Recorded by at-Tirmithī; verified to be *ḥasan* by al-Albānī (*Ṣaḥīḥ ul-Jāmiʿ* no. 724).

2 The souls of the believers meet all other believers' souls upon their death. They are concerned about those whom they have not met yet, and would rather know that they are still in the *dunyā*, and still have a chance of dying as believers, than to know that they had died as disbelievers.

(future) abode." He is then left in the grave, and (the time passes) as if it is but a nap.

And when death descends upon an enemy of Allāh, and he witnesses things (implying his imminent punishment), he wishes that his soul would never depart, and Allāh hates to meet him.

When he is made to sit in his grave, he is asked, "Who is your lord?" He replies, "I do not know." He is told, "May you never know!" A door is then opened from his grave to Hell, and he is hit a blow that can be heard by every creature except the human beings and the *jinns*. And he is told, "Go to sleep like a bitten person." And his grave is made tight on him.›

Abū Hurayrah was asked, "What is a bitten person?" He replied, "One who is bitten by creatures and snakes." [1]

7. Anas's First *Ḥadīth*

Anas (ﷺ) reported that Allāh's Messenger (ﷺ) said:

‹Verily, when a believer is placed in his grave, an angel comes to him and asks him, "What did you worship?" If Allāh guides him, he replies, "I worshipped Allāh." Then he asks him, "What did you say about this man (Muḥammad)?" He answers, "He is Allāh's *ʿabd* and Messenger."

He is not questioned about anything else after this. He is taken to a house in the Fire, and is told, "This would have been your house in the Fire; but Allāh protected you and had mercy upon you; thus He substituted it for you with a house in *Jannah*."

1 Recorded by al-Bazzār; verified to be authentic by al-Albānī (*aṣ-Ṣaḥīḥah* no. 2628).

He says, "Allow me to go give this good news to my family." But he is told, "Be tranquil."

When a disbeliever is put into his grave, an angel comes to him, rebukes him, and asks him, "What did you worship?" He replies, "I do not know." He is told, "You did not know; nor did you recite (*Qur'ān*)!" He is then asked, "What did you say about this man?" He replies, "I said what the people said." He (the angel) then hits him with an iron hammer between his ears; and he emits a shriek which is heard by all creatures except the human beings and *jinns*.› [1]

8. Anas's Second *Ḥadīth*

Anas (☼) reported that Allāh's Messenger (☼) said:

‹Verily, after a '*abd* is placed in his grave, and his companions walk away from him, so that he can hear the echo of their footsteps, two angels come to him. They make him sit, and ask him, "What did you saying about this man (Muḥammad)?"

A believer replies, "I bear witness that he is Allāh's '*abd* and Messenger." He is then told, "Look at your place in the Fire; Allāh has substituted it for you with a place in *Jannah*." Thus he views both of them. His grave is then expanded for him to seventy cubits; and it is filled with greenery until the Day of Resurrection.

As for a disbeliever or a hypocrite, he replies, "I do not know. I said what the people said." He is then told, "You did not know; nor did you recite (*Qur'ān*)!" He is then hit one blow between his ears

1 Recorded by Abū Dāwūd; verified to be authentic by al-Albānī (*Ṣaḥīḥ ul-Jāmi'* no. 1930).

with an iron hammer; and he emits a shriek which is heard by all creatures near him except *jinns* and human beings. His grave contracts on him until his ribs break.› [1]

1 Al-Bukhārī and Muslim.

CHAPTER 3

THE MOMENT OF DEATH

Introduction

In this chapter, we present the incidents that take place from the time that one is on the verge of death, until one's soul starts its trip to the heavens. The incidents are segmented to make it easy for the reader to follow.

With the approach of death, a believer is pleased because the material barrier is about to dissolve, and he is therefore about to meet his Lord. His soul departs with ease, emitting beautiful odors that delight the angels. A disbeliever, on the other hand, is terrified to realize that his great punishment is eminent. His soul is extracted from his body by force, emitting the most loathsome odors.

It is important to note that most of the available texts compare the situation of a believer to that of a disbeliever, without making reference to a sinful believer. Because of this we assume that, in this comparison, a "believer" is one whose good deeds overweigh his sins, so that he will not be punished in the grave or on the Day of Judgement.

As for the believers who have been so sinful as to deserve punishment before they enter *Jannah*, they may be punished in their graves, and possibly after resurrection as well. Their punishment has not been fully detailed in the *Sunnah*. Yet, some of its forms have been described by the Prophet (ﷺ). This is covered in Chapter 8 titled, "The Sinful in *al-Barzakh*".

The following table compares what happens, in each case or situation, to a believer and a disbeliever. The references are numbered after the long *ḥadīth*s cited in Chapter 2. Other references, marked with a "*", are presented later in this chapter under the section titled, "Related Texts".

Tabulated Events

Action or Event	A Believer	A Disbeliever	Ref.
Angels descend from the heaven to "witness" the death.	They are angels of mercy. Their faces are white and bright like the sun.	They are angels of punishment. They are strong, hulking, with dark faces.	1,4
Things brought by the "witnessing" angels:	They bring a piece of white silk and embalmment from *Jannah*.	They bring coarse fabrics from the Fire.	1,4
Sitting position of the angels:	They sit at the limit of his eyesight.		1
Arrival of the angel of death:	He sits by his head.		1
What the "witnessing" angels say to the soul:	"Depart from the body to Allāh's granted happiness."	"Depart from the body to Allāh's wrath."	4
The angel of death's command to the soul to leave the body:	"Depart, O good and peaceful soul that inhabited a good body."	"Depart, O malicious soul that inhabited a malicious body."	1,2

Action or Event	**A Believer**	**A Disbeliever**	**Ref.**
The angel of death's tidings to the soul:	"Depart to Allāh's forgiveness and pleasure; depart in a praised state; and receive glad tidings of happiness, sweet aromas, and a Lord who is not angry."	"Depart to Allāh's wrath and anger; depart in a condemned state; and receive evil tidings of boiling fluids, dirty wound discharges, and other types of suffering."	1,2
How long does the angel of death say this?	He continues to say this until the soul leaves the body.		2
The soul's departure from the body:	It leaves the body as water flows from the spout of a water skin; the angel of death takes it easily.	It becomes terrified, and clings to the body; the angel of death extracts it by force, causing the veins and nerves to burst.	1
The dying person's feeling about meeting Allāh:	He longs to meet Him and loves that.	He hates to meet Him and fears that.	6

Action or Event	A Believer	A Disbeliever	Ref.
What the person says as his soul leaves his body:	He praises Allāh.	He request to be allowed to return to life.	*, p.4
What happens to the eyesight:	It follows the departing soul.		*
Saying of the angels in the heavens and on earth as the soul leaves the body:	They supplicate for him.	They curse him.	1
The gates to the heavens, and their guardians:	They open for him; their guardians plead Allāh to send this soul in their direction.	They are shut; their guardians plead Allāh to avert this soul from them.	1
Action of the "witnessing" angels after the angel of death takes the soul:	They do not leave it in his hand for as little as the blinking of an eye.		1
Action of the "witnessing" angels after they receive the soul:	They place it in the shroud and embalmment from *Jannah*.	They put it in the fabric from the Fire.	1

Action or Event	A Believer	A Disbeliever	Ref.
Smell emanating from the departing soul:	The best smelling scent of musk that ever existed on the surface of the earth.	The most repugnant odor of a decaying cadaver that ever existed on the surface of the earth.	1,4

Related Texts

Praising Allāh

Ibn ʿAbbās (ﷺ) reported that Allāh's Messenger (ﷺ) said:

> **‹A believer praises Allāh as his soul leaves from between his two sides.›** [1]

The Eyesight Follows the Soul

Umm Salamah (ﷺ) reported that the Prophet (ﷺ) said:

> **‹Indeed, when the soul is taken away, the eyesight follows it.›** [2]

The Wrong-Doers in the Agonies of Death

Allāh (ﷻ) says:

1 Recorded by Aḥmad and others; verified to be authentic by al-Albānī (*Ṣaḥīḥ ul-Jāmiʿ* no. 1931).

2 Muslim and others.

﴿وَلَوْ تَرَىٰٓ إِذِ ٱلظَّـٰلِمُونَ فِي غَمَرَٰتِ ٱلْمَوْتِ وَٱلْمَلَـٰٓئِكَةُ بَاسِطُوٓاْ
أَيْدِيهِمْ أَخْرِجُوٓاْ أَنفُسَكُمُ ٱلْيَوْمَ تُجْزَوْنَ عَذَابَ ٱلْهُونِ بِمَا كُنتُمْ
تَقُولُونَ عَلَى ٱللَّهِ غَيْرَ ٱلْحَقِّ وَكُنتُمْ عَنْ ءَايَـٰتِهِ تَسْتَكْبِرُونَ ۝﴾

الأنعام ٩٣

«If you could but see when the wrong-doers are in the agonies of death, and the angels stretching out their hands (and saying), "Deliver your souls! This day you shall be recompensed with the torment of degradation because of what you used to utter against Allāh other than the truth, and you used to reject His āyāt with disrespect.» [1]

1 *Al-An'ām* 6:93.

CHAPTER 4

TRIP TO THE HEAVENS AND BACK

Introduction

After departing from the bodies, the souls are taken up on a trip to the heavens. The believers' souls are warmly welcomed, and are admitted into all of the heavens. They meet the souls of other believers and receive their Lord's praise before returning into the bodies. The disbelievers' souls are condemned, and are not allowed to enter the heavens. They receive their Lord's blame before falling into the bodies. These incidents are detailed in the following table.

The numbered references refer to the *ḥadīth*s in Chapter 2. The "*" references are cited toward the end of this chapter.

Event	A Believer	A Disbeliever	Ref.
Supplication of the angels in the heavens:	"A good soul is coming from the earth; may the blessings of Allāh be upon you and the body that you had inhabited."	"An evil soul is coming from the earth."	*
Who takes the soul up to the heavens:	The "witnessing" angels ascend with it.		1

Event	A Believer	A Disbeliever	Ref.
Smelling the soul's musky aroma:	The angels pass it from one to the next to smell it.	(Not applicable.)	4
What angel gatherings ask along the way to the heavens:	"What is this good soul?"	"What is this malicious soul?"	1
The "witnessing" angels' response:	"He is so and so, son of so and so," uttering the best names with which he had been known.	"He is so and so, son of so and so," uttering the worst names with which he had been known.	1,2
Requesting admission to the heavens:	When they reach the lowest heaven, they ask for permission to enter.		1,2
Reception by the angels guarding the lowest heaven's gates:	"Welcome, good soul that inhabited a good body; enter in a praised state; and receive glad tidings of happiness, sweet aromas, and a Lord who is not angry."	"Unwelcome, malicious soul that inhabited a malicious body; return in a condemned state, because the gates to the heavens will not open for you."	2

Event	A Believer	A Disbeliever	Ref.
Admission of the soul into the heavens:	The gates open for it; it is admitted into al of the heavens.	The gates are shut, and it is not admitted, even into the lowest heaven.	1,2
Reception by the angels guarding the upper heavens' gates:	The soul is welcomed in every heaven, until it reaches the seventh, above which is Allāh's Throne.	(Not applicable.)	1,2
The angels' amazement at the beauty of the soul's scent:	At the gate to each heaven, they ask, "What is this beautiful scent coming from the earth?"	(Not applicable.)	4
Escorts between the heavens:	The most elite angels of each heaven escort it to the next one.	(Not applicable.)	1
Meeting of the soul with the believers' souls:	The angels take it to the souls of the believers.	(Not applicable.)	4,6

Event	A Believer	A Disbeliever	Ref.
Reception by the believers' souls:	They are happier in seeing it than are those to whom a dear one returns from a long absence.	(Not applicable.)	4
Writing the records:	Allāh says, "Write My servant's records in *'Illiyyūn*"	Allāh says, "Write his record in *Sijjīn* in the lowest earth."	1
Allāh's command to the "witnessing" angels to return the soul:	"Take him back to the earth to complete its appointed time before resurrection. I promised them that from it I create them, into it I return them, and from it I resurrect them once again."		1,*
Return to the body:	His soul is returned to the body.	His soul is cast down from the heavens without regard; it falls into his body in the grave.	1,2
Hearing the people's footsteps:	He hears the thumping of his companions' shoes as they walk away from his grave.		1
The squeeze of the grave:	No one is spared it.		*

Related Texts

Squeeze of the Grave

No human being will be spared the squeeze of the grave. However, the following *ḥadīth* indicates that it is not at the same degree of severity for all people; some of the believers are released from its grip quicker than others. Ibn ʿAbbās (ﷺ) said that Allāh's Messenger (ﷺ) said:

> **‹If anyone were to escape from the squeeze of the grave, it would be Saʿd Bin Muʿāth; however, he was squeezed once and then released.›** [1]

The Angels' Supplication for the Believers

Abū Hurayrah (ﷺ) reported that Allāh's Messenger (ﷺ) said:

> **‹When the soul of a believer departs from the body, it is taken by two angels who rise with it (here he (ﷺ) described the sweetness of its fragrance). The inhabitants of the heaven say, "A good soul is coming from the direction of the earth; may Allāh's blessings be upon you and upon the body that you had inhabited." He is then taken to his Lord, Who says, "Take it to complete its appointed time (before resurrection)."**
>
> **But when the soul of a disbeliever departs from the body (here he (ﷺ) described its foul odor), the inhabitants of the heaven say, "An evil soul is coming from the direction of the earth." Then it is said, "Take it to complete its appointed time."›** [2]

1 Aṭ-Ṭabarānī in *al-Kabīr*; *Ṣaḥīḥ ul-Jāmiʿ* by al-Albānī No. 5306.
2 Muslim.

CHAPTER 5

THE FINAL TEST

Introduction

The soul returns to the body after the burial, just in time for the "Final Test". Two very stern angels conduct the test. They ask the soul questions that test the person's level of belief and adherence to the Prophet (ﷺ). With firm words, a believer provides the correct answers, whereas a disbeliever stutters and provides wrong answers. These incidents are detailed in this chapter.

The numbered references in the following table refer to the *ḥadīth*s in Chapter 2. The "*" references are cited later in this chapter.

Tabulated Events

Event	**A Believer**	**A Disbeliever**	**Ref.**
When the test starts:	Immediately after burial.		*
Who conducts the test:	Two angels.		1,5,7, 8
Appearance of the two angels:	They are black and blue, with a very stern appearance.		1,5
Names of the two angels:	Their names are "Munkar" and "Nakīr".		5
First thing done by the angels:	They shake him and make him sit up in his grave.		1,6,8, *

Event	A Believer	A Disbeliever	Ref.
State of anticipation before the test:	He sits without fear or terror.	He sits in a state of fear and terror.	2,3
Manner of answering the questioning:	He says what he used to say (before death). The faculty of reason is returned to him.		5,*
They ask him, "Who is you Lord?"	He replies, "My Lord is Allāh."	He replies, "Alas, alas, I do not know!"	1,6
They ask him, "What is your *Dīn*? What did you say about *Islām*? What did you do?"	He replies, "My *Dīn* is *Islām*. I adhered to it, read Allāh's Book, believed and obeyed it."	He replies, "Alas, alas, I do not know! I heard the people say things; so I said the same."	1,2,3, 6
They ask him, "What did you worship?"	He replies, "I worshipped Allāh."	He replies, "I do not know."	7
His response to the question, "Who is that man who was sent to you?"	"He is Allāh's *'abd* and Messenger Muḥammad. He brought clear signs from Allāh, and we believed him. I testify that there is no (true) god but Allāh, and that Muḥammad is His *'abd* and Messenger."	He cannot recall his name. He is told, "(His name is) Muḥammad!" He says, "Alas, alas, I do not know. I just heard the people say that."	1,2,3, 5,6,8, *

Event	A Believer	A Disbeliever	Ref.
What the angels expected:	"We expected you to say this."		5
Performance in the test:	Allāh guides him and makes him firm in words, so that he knows how to answer his questions.	He is confused and is told, "You did not know, or recite (*Qur'ān*)!"	1,8,*
They shake him again, asking, "Who is your Lord? What is your *Dīn*? Who is your Prophet?"	He repeats, "My Lord is Allāh, my *Dīn* is *Islām*, and my Prophet is Muḥammad."	(Not applicable.)	1
Last *fitnah*:	This is the last *fitnah* to which he is subjected.	(Not applicable.)	1,7
The test's result is announced with a call from the heavens:	"My *'abd* has spoken the truth; give him furnishings from *Jannah*; clothe him from it; and open for him a door to it."	"He lies! Give him furnishings from the Fire; and open for him a door to it."	1

Related Texts

'Uthmān (⚘) narrated that after Allāh's Messenger (⚘) buried a person, he (⚘) would stand by the grave and say:

> ‹Ask Allāh to grant to your brother forgiveness and firmness (of words), because he is being questioned at this moment.› [1]

As death approached him, 'Amr Bin al-'Āṣ (⚘) said to his companions:

> "After you bury me, stand around my grave for as long as it takes to slaughter a camel and distribute its meat; I will thus be comforted by your presence while I am considering how to respond to my Lord's Messengers (the two angels)." [2]

ALLĀH GRANTS FIRMNESS OF WORDS TO THE BELIEVERS

Al-Barā' Bin 'Āzib (⚘) reported that Allāh's Messenger (⚘) said:

> ‹When the believer is placed in the grave, he is made to sit, and is approached (by the two angels); he then testifies that there is no deity (worthy of being worshipped) but Allāh, and that Muḥammad is the Messenger of Allāh. This is why Allāh says:

﴿يُثَبِّتُ ٱللَّهُ ٱلَّذِينَ ءَامَنُواْ بِٱلْقَوْلِ ٱلثَّابِتِ فِي ٱلْحَيَوٰةِ ٱلدُّنْيَا وَفِي ٱلْآخِرَةِ﴾ إبراهيم ٢٧

---

1 Recorded by Abū Dāwūd and al-Ḥākim; verified to be authentic by al-Albānī (*Ṣaḥīḥ ul-Jāmi'* no. 945).
2 Muslim.

«Allāh makes the believers firm with firm words.» [1], [2]

PRESERVING THE FACULTY OF REASON

ʿAbdullāh Bin ʿUmar (ﷺ) reported that Allāh's Messenger (ﷺ) mentioned the questioners (the two angels) of the grave. ʿUmar asked, "Is our reason preserved with us then, O Messenger of Allāh?" He (ﷺ) said, ‹**Yes, as is your present state.**› ʿUmar (ﷺ) then said:

> "I would then throw a stone into his (the angel's) mouth [3]." [4]

1 *Ibrāhīm* 14:27.

2 Al-Bukhārī.

3 This is an Arabic expression which means, "My answer will be so convincing that he will be dumbfound."

4 *Ṣaḥīḥ ut-Targhībi wat-Tarhīb* by al-Albānī Vol. 4.

CHAPTER 6

AFTER THE TEST

Introduction

The test confirms what the person had already realized from the moment of his death. A believer is immediately rewarded with an opening that appears from his grave to *Jannah*. His good deeds materialize next to him in the form of a pleasant looking man. On the other hand, a disbeliever is severely punished, and an opening appears from his grave to Hell. His evil deeds materialize in the form of a repulsive man. These incidents are detailed in this chapter.

The numbered references in the following table refer to the *ḥadīth*s in Chapter 2. The "*" references are cited later in this chapter.

Where the Souls Really Are

It is important to note that some texts indicate that the believers' souls turn into birds in *Jannah*. Other texts indicate that the souls are sometimes attached to the bodies that are in the grave. There is no contradiction between the two situations, because this is a matter of *ghayb* that cannot be subjected to the reasoning deriving from our worldly experience. A good example to facilitate understanding this is the dreams that take place during our sleep, where our souls seem to make trips to worlds beyond human perception.

Ibn ul-Qayyim has a very detailed discussion regarding this and related issues in his book *ar-Rūḥ* (the Soul). We quote from it the following:

> "The soul's attachment to the body has five different stages:
>
> a) Its attachment to it while it is still an embryo in the mother's womb.

b) Its attachment to it after it emerges to the surface of the earth.
c) Its attachment to it during sleep. In that case, it is attached to it in one respect, and detached in another respect.
d) Its attachment to it in *al-Barzakh*. Even though it departs and becomes detached from it, its detachment is not complete so as to have absolutely no connection with it.
e) Its attachment to it on the Day of Reckoning, which is the most complete and inseparable attachment …"

Tabulated Events

Event	A Believer	A Disbeliever	Ref.
Furnishings and clothing:	He is given furnishings and clothes from *Jannah*.	He is given furnishings from the Fire.	1
Openings from the grave to future abodes:	Two openings appear in it: One to *Jannah*; and he views its grandeur and bounties. The other to the Fire; and he sees its various sections crushing each other.		1,2,3
Seeing, from his grave, the place that he evaded:	Pointing to the Fire, the angels tell him, "This could have been your place, had you disobeyed Allāh; but Allāh has saved you from it."	Pointing to *Jannah*, the angels tell him, "Look at that from which Allāh has deprived you."	1,2,3, 7,8

Event	A Believer	A Disbeliever	Ref.
Seeing, from his grave, his final destination:	He sees his future place in *Jannah*, tastes its provision and perfume, and is told, "Allāh has granted you this place in it."	He sees his future place in the Fire, tastes its heat and fierce hot wind, and is told, "This will be your abode in it."	1,2,3, 6,7,8
Between doubt and certitude:	He is told, "You lived with certitude; upon it you died; and upon it you will be raised – when Allāh wills."	He is told, "In doubt you lived; upon it you died; and upon it you will be raised – when Allāh wills."	2,3
Extent of the grave:	It is spread to the extent of his eyesight – seventy cubits by seventy.	The earth is told, "Contract on him." And it contracts until his ribs break.	1,5,6, 8
Light in the grave:	It is illuminated for him because of the Prophet's supplication.	Darkness engulfs him.	5,*
Greenery in the grave:	It is filled with greenery until the Day of Resurrection.	(Not applicable.)	8

Event	A Believer	A Disbeliever	Ref.
Companion in the grave:	His good deeds take the form of a good looking, nicely dressed, and pleasantly smelling person.	His bad deeds take the form of an ugly looking, hideously dressed, and foully smelling person.	1
Tidings carried by the companion:	"I am to give you glad tidings of Allāh's acceptance, and gardens with everlasting bliss. This is the day that you have been promised."	"I am to give you evil tidings. This is the day that you have been promised."	1
Response of the dead person to the companion:	"Glad tidings from Allāh be to you too. Who are you? Your face is one that brings goodness."	"Evil tidings from Allāh be to you too! Who are you? Your face is one that brings evil."	1
Explanation by the companion:	"I am your good deeds. By Allāh, I only knew you quick in obeying Allāh, and slow in disobeying Him. May He reward you with good."	"I am your malicious deeds. By Allāh, I only knew you slow in obeying Allāh, and quick in disobeying Him. May He repay you with evil."	1

Event	**A Believer**	**A Disbeliever**	**Ref.**
Executor in the grave:	(Not applicable.)	A blind, deaf, and dumb person is appointed for him. He has an iron hammer that can turn mountains to dust.	1
Beating in the grave:	(Not applicable.)	He is hit between his ears, once and again, each time turning to dust, and getting restored as he was.	1,7,8
Uncanny shrieks of agony:	(Not applicable.)	His shrieks are heard by everything (even animals) except the human beings and the *jinns*.	1,7,8, *
Wish of the dead regarding resurrection, when they see what awaits them:	"My Lord, speed up the Resurrection, so that I may rejoin my family and property."	"My Lord! Do not establish the Hour."	1,5,7

Event	A Believer	A Disbeliever	Ref.
Wish to return:	"Allow me to go give this good news to my family."	(Not applicable.)	5,7
Response of the two angels to the wish:	"Calm down; sleep as does a newlywed person, whom no one awakens except the member of his family who is dearest to him."	(Not applicable.)	1,5,7
The rest of the abode in *al-Barzakh*:	He sleeps until Allāh raises him from his resting place.	He sleeps like a bitten person, and his punishment goes on.	5,6
Where the soul stays until the Day of Resurrection:	His soul is turned into a bird that eats from the trees of *Jannah*.	(No information.)	*
Showing him his future abode morning and evening:	He is shown his place in *Jannah*, and is told, "This will be your place when Allāh raises you on the Day of Resurrection."		*

Related Texts

CONTINUAL EXPOSITION TO THE FUTURE POSITION

Allāh (ﷻ) says:

﴿ٱلنَّارُ يُعْرَضُونَ عَلَيْهَا غُدُوًّا وَعَشِيًّا وَيَوْمَ تَقُومُ ٱلسَّاعَةُ أَدْخِلُوٓا۟ ءَالَ فِرْعَوْنَ أَشَدَّ ٱلْعَذَابِ۝﴾ غافر ٤٦

«The Fire; they (the people of Pharaoh) are exposed to it morning and evening; and on the Day when the Hour will be established (it will be said to the angels): "Let Pharaoh's people into the severest torment."» [1]

Ibn ʿUmar (ﷺ) said that Allāh's Messenger (ﷺ) said:

‹When one of you dies, he is shown his (future) position morning and evening. If he is from the people of *Jannah*, (he is shown his place) in *Jannah*, and if he is from the people of the Fire, (he is shown his place) in the Fire; and each is told, "This will be your place when Allāh raises you on the Day of Resurrection."› [2]

SCREAMS OF AGONY

Ibn Masʿūd (ﷺ) said that Allāh's Messenger (ﷺ) said:

‹Verily, the dead are punished in their graves, and even the animals hear their screaming.› [3]

1 *Ghāfir* 40:46.

2 Al-Bukhārī and Muslim.

3 Recorded by Abū Nuʿaym and aṭ-Ṭabarānī in *al-Kabīr*; verified to be authentic by al-Albānī (*Ṣaḥīḥ ul-Jāmiʿ* no. 1965).

Zayd Bin Thābit (⬤) reported that Allāh's Messenger (⬤) said:

> ⟨Verily, those people (the dead) are being afflicted in the grave. Were it not that you may tend to stop burying each other, I would have asked Allāh (⬤) to let you hear the torture of the grave as I do.⟩ [1]

DARKNESS IN THE GRAVE

Abū Hurayrah and Anas (⬤) reported that Allāh's Messenger (⬤) said:

> ⟨Indeed, these graves engulf their dwellers with darkness; and verily Allāh illuminates them (for the believers) because of my ṣalāh (supplication) for them.⟩ [2]

EATING FROM THE TREES OF JANNAH

Kaʿb Bin Mālik narrated that Allāh's Messenger (⬤) said:

> ⟨Verily, a believer's soul is (turned into) a bird that eats from the trees of Jannah until Allāh (⬤) sends it to his body on the day that it will be resurrected.⟩ [3]

---

1 Muslim and Aḥmad.
2 Muslim and others.
3 Recorded by Mālik, Aḥmad, and others; verified to be authentic by al-Albānī (Ṣaḥīḥ ul-Jāmiʿ no. 2373).

CHAPTER 7

THE PROPHETS AND THE MARTYRS

Introduction

The prophets, the martyrs, and the most righteous believers have a special well-earned status in the hereafter. This applies to *al-Barzakh* as well. The prophets' bodies are preserved from decay, and they live a special type of life in which they continuously pray to their Lord (ﷻ). The martyrs' souls are with the other believers' souls in *Jannah*, but their souls are within green birds, and they are closer to Allāh, being immediately under the Throne.

Preservation of the Prophets' Bodies

The earth does not consume the bodies of the Prophets. Aws Bin Aws (ﷺ) narrated that Allāh's Messenger (ﷺ) said:

> **‹Indeed, among the best of all of your days is the day of *Jumu'ah* (Friday). On such a day, Ādam was created, he died, on it the blow (of the *Ṣūr* or trumpet of the Doom's Hour) will be sounded, and on it is the great shock (when all those on earth will die following the blow of the *Ṣūr*); so say in plenty your *salāh* upon me on Friday, for indeed your *ṣalāh* will be presented to me. Indeed, Allāh has prohibited the earth from eating up the bodies of prophets.›** [1]

1 Recorded by Aḥmad, Abū Dāwūd and others; verified to be authentic by al-Albānī (*Ṣaḥīḥ ul-Jāmi'* no. 2212).

The Prophets' Life in Their Graves

The Prophets live and pray in their graves. However, their life is not the life of this world, but is a life from *al-Barzakh*. What distinguishes it from the life of the other believers is that the latter sleep in their graves, whereas the prophets are granted the ability and merit to continue to pray even after death. Anas Bin Mālik (رضي الله عنه) reported that Allāh's Messenger (ﷺ) said:

> **‹The prophets are alive in their graves; and they are praying (therein).›** [1]

Anas (رضي الله عنه) also reported that the Messenger (ﷺ) said:

> **‹On the night of *Isrā'* [2], I passed by Mūsā, who was standing in prayer in his grave.›** [3]

Some scholars, such as al-Manāwī, believe that this *ḥadīth* refers to the original linguistic meaning of the prayer, "It means that he was making *du'ā'*, praising Allāh, and mentioning Him." [4] Others, such as al-Qurṭubī, believe that it refers to the actual *shar'ī* (legislated) prayer.

Note that there is no conflict between this *ḥadīth* and that (cited below) in which the Prophet (ﷺ) says that he also saw Mūsā (عليه السلام) on that night in the Sixth Heaven. The latter one refers to Mūsā's soul, whereas the first one refers to his body joined by the soul in a *ghaybī* manner. [5]

Conveying the *Ṣalāh*

Allāh (ﷻ) appoints an angel at the grave of Allāh's Messenger (ﷺ) to inform him, by name, of each one who says the *ṣalāh* upon him. Abū Bakr (رضي الله عنه) reported that Allāh's Messenger (ﷺ) said:

1 Recorded by Abū Y'alā, al-Bazzār and others; verified to be authentic by al-Albānī (*Ṣaḥīḥ ul-Jāmi'* no. 2790).

2 *Isrā'*: The Prophet's (ﷺ) miraculous night trip from Makkah to Jerusalem.

3 Muslim and others.

4 *Fayḍ ul-Qadīr* 5:519.

5 *Al-Āyāt ul-Bayyināt* 41.

‹Say the ṣalāh upon me frequently, because Allāh has appointed for me an angel who stays by my grave. Whenever one of my *Ummah* (Nation or followers) says the ṣalāh upon me, that angel says to me, "O Muḥammad, such and such person said the ṣalāh upon you at this moment."› [1]

Also, Abū Masʿūd al-Anṣārī (⬥) reported that the Messenger (⬥) also said:

‹Say the ṣalāh upon me plentifully on *al-Jumuʿah* (Friday), for no one says the ṣalāh upon me on Friday but his ṣalāh is presented to me.› [2]

The Night Journey

Mālik Bin Ṣaʿṣaʿah narrated that Allāh's Messenger (⬥) described to the ṣaḥābah his Night Journey (*al-Isrāʾ* and *al-Miʿrāj*) as follows:

‹While I was lying at al-Ḥaṭīm [3], someone suddenly came to me and cut my body open from here to here [4] and took out my heart. A gold washbowl full of *Īmān* (faith) was then brought to me. My heart was washed with *Zamzam*'s water and filled with *Īmān*; it was then returned to its original place.

Before me was brought an animal smaller than a mule and larger than a donkey, white in color, called *al-Burāq*. (It travels so fast that) it places its footstep

---

1 Recorded by ad-Daylamī; verified to be *hasan* by al-Albānī (*Ṣaḥīḥ ul-Jāmiʿ* no. 1207).

2 Recorded by al-Ḥākim and al-Bayhaqī; verified to be authentic by al-Albānī (*Ṣaḥīḥ ul-Jāmiʿ* no. 1208).

3 The wall of *al-Kaʿbah* nearest to the black stone. It is so called because people crowd around it.

4 From his throat to his navel.

at the end of its eyesight. I was carried on it, and Jibrīl led me till he reached the lowest heaven.

When he requested admission, he was asked, "Who is it?" He said, "Jibrīl." He was asked, "Who accompanies you?" He replied, "Muḥammad." He was asked, "Has he been summoned?" He said, "Yes." It was then said, "He is welcome; what an excellent visit his is!" The gate was opened. When I entered, I saw Ādam (عليه السلام). Jibrīl said, "This is your father, Ādam; so give him *salām* (greeting with peace)." I gave him *salām*. He returned my *salām* and said, "Welcome, righteous Prophet and righteous son."

Jibrīl then ascended with me until we reached the second heaven. He requested admission, and was asked, "Who is it?" He said, "Jibrīl." He was asked, "Who accompanies you?" He replied, "Muḥammad." He was asked, "Has he been summoned?" He said, "Yes." It was then said, "He is welcome; what an excellent visit his is!" The gate was opened. When I entered, I saw Yaḥyā (John) and ʿĪsā (Jesus), who are cousins. Jibrīl said, "These are Yaḥyā and ʿĪsā; give them *salām*." I gave them *salām*. They returned my *salām* and said, "Welcome, righteous brother and righteous prophet."

Jibrīl then ascended with me to the third heaven. He requested admission, and was asked, "Who is it?" He said, "Jibrīl." He was asked, "Who accompanies you?" He replied, "Muḥammad." He was asked, "Has he been summoned?" He said, "Yes." It was then said, "He is welcome; what an excellent visit his is!" The gate was opened. When I entered I saw Yūsuf. Jibrīl said, "This is Yūsuf; give him *salām*." I gave him *salām*. He returned my *salām* and said, "Welcome, righteous brother and righteous prophet."

Jibrīl then ascended with me to the fourth heaven. He requested admission, and was asked,

"Who is it?" He said, "Jibrīl." He was asked, "Who accompanies you?" He replied, "Muḥammad." He was asked, "Has he been summoned?" He said, "Yes." It was then said, "He is welcome; what an excellent visit his is!" The gate was opened. When I entered, I saw Idrīs. Jibrīl said, "This is Idrīs; give him *salām*." I gave him *salām*. He returned my *salām* and said, "Welcome, righteous brother and righteous prophet."

Jibrīl then ascended with me to the fifth heaven. He requested admission, and was asked, "Who is it?" He said, "Jibrīl." He was asked, "Who accompanies you?" He replied, "Muḥammad." He was asked, "Has he been summoned?" He said, "Yes." It was then said, "He is welcome; what an excellent visit his is!" When I entered I saw Hārūn (Aaron). Jibrīl said, "This is Hārūn; give him *salām*." I gave him *salām*. He returned my *salām* and said, "Welcome, righteous brother and righteous prophet."

Jibrīl then ascended with me to the sixth heaven. He requested admission, and was asked, "Who is it?" He said, "Jibrīl." He was asked, "Who accompanies you?" He replied, "Muḥammad." He was asked, "Has he been summoned?" He said, "Yes." It was then said, "He is welcome; what an excellent visit his is!" When I entered I saw Mūsā (Moses). Jibrīl said, "This is Mūsā; give him *salām*." I gave him *salām*. He returned my *salām* and said, "Welcome, righteous brother and righteous prophet." After I passed on, he began crying; he was asked, "What makes you cry?" He said, "I am crying because a young man, sent after me (with the Message from Allāh), has followers who will enter *Jannah* in greater numbers than my followers."

Jibrīl then ascended with me to the seventh heaven. He requested admission, and was asked, "Who is it?" He said, "Jibrīl." He was asked, "Who

accompanies you?" He replied, "Muḥammad." He was asked, "Has he been summoned?" He said, "Yes." It was then said, "He is welcome; what an excellent visit his is!" When I entered I saw Ibrāhīm. Jibrīl said, "This is your father Ibrāhīm; give him *salām*." I gave him *salām*. He responded to my *salām* and said, "Welcome, righteous son and righteous prophet."

I was then shown *Sidrat ul-Muntahā* [1]. And behold! Its fruits were like the jars of Hajar [2], and its leaves were as big as elephants' ears. Jibrīl said, "This is *Sidrat ul-Muntahā*." There ran four rivers, two were concealed and two were visible. I asked, "What are these rivers, O Jibrīl?" He replied, "As for the two concealed ones, they are two rivers in *Jannah*; and as for the two visible ones, they are the Nile and the Euphrates."

Then I was shown *al-Bayt ul-Maʿmūr* [3]. I said, "What is this, O Jibrīl?" He replied, "This is *al-Bayt ul-Maʿmūr*: seventy thousand angels enter into it every day; and once they leave, they never enter it again."

I was then offered a flask of wine, a flask of milk, and a flask of honey. I took the one that contained milk. Jibrīl remarked: "This is the *fiṭrah* [4] upon which you and your followers are."

Fifty *ṣalāhs* (prayers) were then made obligatory for me each day. On my way back I passed by Mūsā, who asked me, "What have you been commanded?" I replied, "I have been commanded to perform fifty prayers each day." Mūsā said, "Your *Ummah* (followers) cannot accomplish fifty prayers each day.

1 *Sidrat ul-Muntahā*: The Lotus Tree at the Farthest Limit, beyond which no one is allowed to pass.

2 Hajar: A village near al-Madīnah where huge clay jars used to be made.

3 *Al-Bayt ul-Maʿmūr*: The Much-Frequented House in the heavens.

4 *Fiṭrah*: The pure nature according to which Allāh created the people.

By Allāh, I have dealt with the people before you; and I tried my utmost with the Children of Isrā'īl. Go back to your Lord, and ask him to reduce the burden for your *Ummah*."

I returned; and Allāh reduced the required number of prayers by ten. Again, I came to Mūsā, who repeated his earlier advise to me.

I returned; and Allāh reduced the number by ten. I came to Mūsā, who repeated his earlier advise.

I returned; and Allāh reduced the number by ten. I came to Mūsā, who repeated his earlier advise.

I returned; and Allāh reduced the number by ten, thus commanding me to perform ten prayers each day. And Mūsā repeated his earlier advise.

I returned, and was commanded to perform five prayers each day. When I cam back to Mūsā, He said, "What have you been commanded?" I replied, "I have been commanded to perform five prayers each day." He said, "Your *Ummah* cannot accomplish five prayers each day. I have dealt with the people before you; and I tried my utmost with the Children of Isrā'īl. Go back to your Lord, and ask him to reduce the burden for your *Ummah*." I said, I have requested so much from my Lord that I now feel shy (to ask anymore of Him). I will just accept this and submit to Him. As I left, I heard a caller address me by saying, "You have submitted to My command, and have reduced the burden for My worshippers."› [1]

The Martyred

The companions of the Prophet (ﷺ) who were martyred in the battle of *Uḥud* are anxious to inform their brothers about what Allāh (ﷻ) has

1 Al-Bukhārī, Muslim and others.

granted the martyrs. Ibn ʿAbbās (ﷺ) narrated that Allāh's Messenger (ﷺ) said:

> **‹When your brothers were killed in the battle of *Uḥud*, Allāh (ﷻ) cast their ʿsouls into green birds that frequent the rivers of *Jannah*, eat of its fruits, and rest in lamps of gold hanging in the shadow of the *ʿArsh* [1]. When they found this pleasant food, drink, and repose, they said, "Who will inform our brothers, on our behalf, that we are alive in *Jannah,* and that we receive sustenance – so that they do not forsake *jihād* (fighting in Allāh's way) or turn back during the fighting?" Allāh (ﷻ) said, "I will inform them for you."›** [2]

1 *ʿArsh*: Throne.

2 Recorded by Aḥmad, Abū Dāwūd and al-Ḥākim; verified to be authentic by al-Albānī (*Ṣaḥīḥ ul-Jāmiʿ* no. 5205).

CHAPTER 8

THE SINFUL IN *AL-BARZAKH*

Samurah's *Ḥadīth*

Samurah Bin Jundub (☙) reported that Allāh's Messenger (☙) would often inquire from his companions, ‹**Did anyone of you see a dream this night?**› So dreams would be narrated to him by those whom Allāh wills them to do. One morning he (☙) told them:

> ‹Last night two men came to me (in a dream [1]) and said, "Come with us." I went with them to a sacred land.
>
> 1) We came upon a man lying flat on his back (on the ground). Another man was standing over his head with a boulder in his hand. He would hurl the boulder upon the (first) man's head, causing it to split open. The boulder would then roll away, and he would go and retrieve it. By the time he returned to him, his head is restored as it was before, and he would hit him again (with the boulder). I said to them, "May Allāh be exalted! Who are these two?" They said, "Come on, come on!"
>
> 2) We proceeded until we came upon a man sitting, and another man standing over him with an iron hook. He would approach him from one side, and rip open (with the hook) his face from the corner of the mouth to the back of the head, from the nose to the back of the head, and from the eye to the back of

---

1   The prophets' dreams are all truthful; Satan cannot approach them even while they sleep.

the head. He would then move to the other side and do what he did on the first side. As soon as he finished with that side, the first side would be restored to what it was before, and he would move to it and do as he did the first time. I said, "May Allāh be exalted! Who are these two?" They said, "Come one, come on!"

3) We proceeded until we came upon a hole that resembled a baking pit, narrow at the top and wide at the bottom. Babbling and voices were issuing from it. We looked in and saw naked men and women. Underneath the pit was a raging fire; whenever it flared up, they screamed and rose with it until they almost fell out of the pit. As it subsided, they returned (to the bottom). I said, "Who are these?" They said, "Come on; come on!"

4) We proceeded until we reached a river of blood, with a man swimming in its center. On the bank of the river there was a man who had piled around him many rocks. The man in the river would swim for a while, and then approach the one who had gathered the rocks around him, trying to exit (from the river). He would open his mouth, and he (the one standing on the bank) would throw a rock into it, causing him to return to his original position (in the middle of the river). He would then resume swimming; and every time he made an effort to get out (of the river), he would throw a rock into his mouth, forcing him to fall back to the center. I said, "Who are these two?" They said, "Come on, come on!"

5) We proceeded until we came upon a garden dense with plantation, with all sorts of spring flowers, and with a very large tree in its center. Near the stem of the tree, there stood a very tall man – so tall that I could barely see his head in the sky. Around him

was the greatest number of children that I have ever seen. I said, “Who is this, and who are these?” They said, “Come on, come on!”

6) Near the tree, I saw a man with the most hateful appearance in any man. Before him was a fire, which he was kindling and trotting around. I said to them, “Who is this?” They said, “Come on; come on!”

7) As for the tree, never before had I seen a tree greater or more beautiful than this one. They instructed me, “Climb it.” We ascended, until we came upon a city that I have never seen one more beautiful. It was built with gold and silver bricks. We arrived at the gate of the city and requested admission. It was opened, and we entered into it. We were met by old and young men with one half of their faces the most beautiful to behold, and the other half the ugliest to behold. They (my two companions) said to them, “Go and plunge into that river.” A river was flowing across, whose water was milk-white in color. They plunged into it and returned to us. Their ugliness disappeared; and they became most handsome.

8) They took me further up, and let me into a town better and more beautiful than the first one.

I said, “Since the beginning of this night, you have taken me to different places, and I have been seeing amazing things! What is all this that I saw?” They said, “We will now tell you:

1) As for the first man whom you saw his head getting smashed with a boulder: he is a man whom Allāh taught the *Qur’ān,* but he slept and neglected

it during the night, and did not implement it during the day. He turned away from the *Qur'ān,* and slept through the prescribed prayers. He will continue to be tortured in this way until the Day of Resurrection.

2) As for the man whom you saw with his mouth, nose, and eyes being ripped to the back of his head: he is a liar who leaves his house in the morning to spread lies which are carried from him in all directions. He will continue to be tortured in this way until the Day of Resurrection.

3) As for the naked men and women who were in the pit: they are men and women who indulge in *zinā* (adultery).

4) As for the man whom you saw swimming in the river and being fed with rocks: he is the one who eats *ribā* [1].

5) As for the tall man that you saw in the garden, he is Ibrāhīm (ﷺ). The children about him are all those children who have died according to *fiṭrah* [2].

(Here, some of the companions interjected, 'O Messenger of Allāh! The children of the disbelievers too?' He (ﷺ) said, ‹The children of the disbelievers as well!›)

6) As for the man with extremely ugly appearance who was by the fire, kindling it and running around it: he is Mālik, the Guardian of *Jahannam* (Hell).

1 Eating *ribā* means to take usury or deal with any prohibited transactions. Unfortunately, many such transactions in our time are given deceiving names like "interest" or "benefit". But there is no interest or benefit in them; and the names do not change their reality of being major sins and pure harm.

2 *Fiṭrah* is the pure and clean nature according to which all people are born before they are influenced by their societies and upbringing.

7) As for the first town, it is the dwelling place of the common believers. The people who were half handsome and half ugly: they are people who mixed good with evil deeds, and Allāh forgave them."

8) And as for this town, it is the dwelling place of the *shuhadā* (martyrs).

They added, "I am Jibrīl, and this is Mīkā'īl. This is the Garden of *'Adn* (Eden); and that over there is your residence. Now raise your head." I raised my eyes and saw, above me, a castle that resembled a white cloud. They said (again), "That is your dwelling." I said to them, "May Allāh bless you; allow me to enter my dwelling." They said, "Not yet! There is a portion of your life which you have not yet completed; when you complete it, you will surely enter your dwelling." ›[1]

Sins Punishable in the Grave

In the following table, we summarize the sins that were specifically mentioned in authentic texts as being punishable in *al-Barzakh*. In the column of references, "S" refers to the above *hadīth* of Samurah (⬥), and "*" refers to the additional *hadīth*s appearing later in this chapter.

It is important to note that these texts provide examples of sins that are punished in the grave. However, there could be other punishable sins that we have not been informed about.

---

1   This is a combined narration of two different reports recorded by al-Bukhārī from Samurah.

Sinful Person	Punishment in *al-Barzakh*	Ref.
A *kāfir*.	Being the worst sin, his punishment is the most sever, as detailed in earlier chapters.	Earlier chaps.
One who rejects the *Qur'ān* after knowing it, and sleeps through the prescribed prayers.	He lies on his back on the ground. A man smashes his head, once and again, with a boulder.	S
A liar who spreads lies which are carried from him in all directions.	His mouth, nose, and eyes are continuously ripped, with a sharp hook, to the back of his head.	S
Men and women who indulge in *zinā* (adultery).	They are put, naked, into a hole that resembles a baking pit, narrow at the top and wide at the bottom. Underneath the pit is a raging fire; whenever it flares up, they scream and rise with it until they almost fall out of the pit. As it subsided, they return (to the bottom).	S
One who take *ribā* (usury).	He swims in a river of blood, on whose bank stands a man with a pile of rock. Every time he tries to exit from the river, the man throws a rock into his mouth, causing him to fall back to the center of the river.	S
One who does not clean himself from traces of urine.	This is the most common reason of punishment; but it is not specified what form of punishment he receives.	*

Sinful Person	Punishment in *al-Barzakh*	Ref.
One whose relatives wail or weep over him (expressing dissatisfaction with Allāh's decree).	He receives punishment (unspecified), or his punishment is increased. This applies to a disbeliever, as well as a believer who had encouraged his relatives to do so.	*
One whose relatives are excessive in praising him.	Allāh appoints two angels who hit him in the neck saying, "Were you like that?"	*
One who spreads *namīmah* (slander) among the people.	This is one of the great sin punished in *al-Barzakh*. Its punishment is not specified.	*

Additional Texts

Contamination with Urine

Ibn ʿAbbās (ﷺ) reported that Allāh's Messenger (ﷺ) said:

> **‹The most prevalent punishment of the grave is because of urine.›** [1]

Wailing of a Disbeliever's Relatives

ʿĀ'ishah (ﷺ) reported that Allāh's Messenger (ﷺ) said:

> **‹Indeed Allāh increases the punishment of a disbeliever because of the weeping of some members of his family over him.›** [2]

1 Recorded by al-Ḥākim; verified to be authentic by al-Albānī (*Ṣaḥīḥ ul-Jāmiʿ* no. 3971).

2 Recorded by an-An-Nasā'ī; verified to be authentic by al-Albānī (*Ṣaḥīḥ ul-Jāmiʿ* no.

WAILING OF A DEAD PERSON'S RELATIVES

Any dead person is also liable to the punishment of the grave because of the lamentation over him. He would be excused, however, if he had urged his family during his life not to do so after his death. 'Abdullāh Bin 'Umar (🙪) reported that Allāh's Messenger (🙪) said:

> ‹The dead (person) is punished in his grave because of the wailing over him.› [1]

EXCESSIVENESS IN PRAISING THE DEAD PERSON

Abū Mūsā (🙪) narrated that Allāh's Messenger (🙪) said:

> ‹Whenever a person dies, and one of his mourners stands up and cries, "O you whom we used to rely on! O you who used to rescue us! ...," and so on, two angels are appointed to hit him in the neck saying, "Were you truly as they say?"› [2]

SLANDERING

Ibn 'Abbās (🙪) reported that Allāh's Messenger (🙪) passed by two graves and said:

> ‹Verily, these two (dead people) are being tortured. Their punishment is for matters that are not important (to many people). But they are very serious indeed. As for the first, he used to walk about spreading slander; and as for the other, he did not cover himself from his urine.› [3]

1897).

1   Al-Bukhārī, Muslim and others.
2   Recorded by at-Tirmi<u>th</u>ī; verified to be *hasan* by al-Albānī (*Ṣaḥīḥ ul-Jāmi'* no. 5788).
3   Al-Bukhārī and Muslim.

CHAPTER 9

SAVIORS FROM THE PUNISHMENT

From the previous chapters, it is apparent that the best protection against punishment in the grave is to carry the true belief in Allāh and avoid the major sins. In this chapter, we additionally present specific things that protect from the punishment of the grave.

Martyrdom on the Battlefield

Al-Miqdām Bin Ma'd Yakrib narrated that Allāh's Messenger (ﷺ) said:

> **‹A *shahīd* (martyr) is favored by Allāh with seven qualities:**
>
> **(a) He is forgiven as soon as his blood gushes forth;**
> **(b) he is shown his position in *Jannah*;**
> **(c) he is adorned with the adornments of *Īmān*;**
> **(d) he is married to seventy two wives of *al-Ḥūr ul-'Īn* (fair females with wide lovely eyes);**
> **(e) he is protected from the torment of the grave, and is saved from the Great Fear (on the Day of Judgement);**
> **(f) on his head is placed the crown of dignity, each of whose jewels is better than the world and all what is in it;**
> **(g) and he is allowed to intercede for seventy of his relatives.›** [1]

1 Recorded by at-Tirmithī, Ibn Mājah, and Ahmad; verified to be authentic by al-Albānī (*Ṣaḥīḥ ul-Jāmi'* no. 5182).

One of the companions of the Prophet (ﷺ) reported that a man said, "O Messenger of Allāh, why are all the believers tested in their graves except a martyr?" He (ﷺ) said:

> **‹The flashing of swords over his head was a sufficient *fitnah* (test) for him.›** [1]

Standing Guard in the Way of Allāh

Salmān (ﷺ) reported that Allāh's Messenger (ﷺ) said:

> **‹Standing guard (on the battle ground) for one day and night is better than fasting the days and praying the nights of an entire month. And if he (the guard) dies, his (good) deeds that he used to do continue to accumulate for him (until the Day of Judgement); he is provided with his provisions (from *Jannah*); and he is saved from *al-Fattān* [2].›** [3]

Fuḍālah Bin ʿUbayd and ʿUqbah Bin ʿĀmir (ﷺ) reported that Allāh's Messenger (ﷺ) said:

> **‹Every dead person's deeds are sealed (at the time of death), except for the one who stands guard in the way of Allāh: his (good) deeds continue to increase until the Day of Resurrection; and he is protected from the trial of the grave.›** [4]

1 Recorded by an-Nasā'ī; verified to be authentic by al-Albānī (*Ṣaḥīḥ ul-Jāmiʿ* no. 4483).

2 *Al-Fattān*: The angel who test people in the grave.

3 Muslim.

4 Recorded by Aḥmad, Abū Dāwūd, at-Tirmi<u>th</u>ī, and others; verified to be authentic by al-Albānī (*Ṣaḥīḥ ul-Jāmiʿ* no. 4562).

Death Caused by Abdomen Diseases

'Abdullāh Bin Yasār reported that he was sitting with Sulaymān Bin Ṣard and Khālid Bin 'Arfaṭah (🙵). They mentioned that a man died of an abdominal disease; and they expressed desire to witness his funeral; one of them said to the other, "Did Allāh's Messenger (🙵) not say:

> ‹Whoever is killed by a disease in his abdomen will not be punished in the grave?›"

The other one replied, "Yes. You spoke the truth." [1]

Reciting *Sūrat ul-Mulk*

'Abdullāh Bin Mas'ūd (🙵) reported that Allāh's Messenger (🙵) said:

> ‹*Sūrat Tabārak* is the protector from the torment of the grave.› [2]

Dying on Friday

'Abdullāh Bin 'Amr (🙵) said that Allāh's Messenger (🙵) said:

> ‹For any Muslim who dies on the day or night of *Jumu'ah* (Friday), Allāh protects him from the trial of the grave.› [3]

---

1   Recorded by at-Tirmithī and others; verified to be authentic by al-Albānī in *Aḥkām ul-Janā'iz*.
2   Recorded by Al-Ḥakim and others; verified to be authentic by al-Albānī (*Ṣaḥīḥ ul-Jāmi'* no. 3643).
3   Recorded by Aḥmad and at-Tirmithī; verified to be *ḥasan* by al-Albānī (*Ṣaḥīḥ ul-Jāmi'* no. 5773).

CHAPTER 10

COMMUNICATION WITH *AL-BARZAKH* [1]

The Dead's Ability to Hear?

Do the dead hear what takes place in this world? This question is not subject to human opinions or speculations. It is a matter of *ghayb* that is encompassed by Allāh's knowledge, and may only be established through a clear evidence from Allāh's book and His Messenger's (ﷺ) *Sunnah.*

The true understanding in this regard is that the dead cannot, in general, hear what takes place on the earth. There are, however, exceptions to this general rule that are established in the Book and the *Sunnah.* We have to accept these exceptional cases and believe in them, without generalizing them beyond their boundaries.

In this chapter, we will establish this understanding by presenting the proper evidence and, in some cases, refuting the wrong evidence used by some people to the contrary.

Comparison with the Deaf

Allāh (ﷻ) says:

﴿إِنَّكَ لَا تُسْمِعُ ٱلْمَوْتَىٰ وَلَا تُسْمِعُ ٱلصُّمَّ ٱلدُّعَآءَ إِذَا وَلَّوْا۟ مُدْبِرِينَ ۝﴾

النمل ٨٠

1 This chapter draws heavily on "*al-Āyāt ul-Bayyināt*" by al-Ālūsī and al-Albānī.

«So, verily (O Muḥammad), you cannot make the dead hear you, nor can you make the deaf hear the call while they turn their backs to you.» [1]

In this *āyah*, Allāh (ﷻ) compares the dead disbelievers to the deaf people. This obviously indicates that they share with them the characteristic of being unable to hear. Ibn Jarīr aṭ-Ṭabarī (رحمه الله) supports this understanding in his *Tafsīr* (*Qurʾānic* commentary) by saying:

> "This is a parable meaning, 'You cannot make these disbelievers understand, because Allāh has sealed their hearing and has taken away their ability to understand the revealed lessons that are recited to them – just as you cannot make the dead understand by giving them hearing, because Allāh has taken away their hearing faculty.'
>
> He is further saying, 'You cannot make the deaf hear after they turn their backs to you, because they have been deprived of the hearing faculty. Similarly, for those whom Allāh has deprived of the ability to hear and understand the *āyāt* of His Book, you cannot help them in hearing and understanding.' " [2]

Aṭ-Ṭabarī then reported that Qatādah (رحمه الله) said:

> "Allāh gives this parable for a *kāfir* (disbeliever). Just as the dead cannot hear the calls, so the *kāfir*s cannot hear. Thus He tells, 'If a deaf person turns his back to you and you call him, he would not hear you. Similarly, a *kāfir* would not hear, nor would he benefit from what he hears.' " [3]

---

1   *An-Naml* 27:80 and *ar-Rūm* 30:52.

2   *Tafsīr aṭ-Ṭabarī* 21:36.

3   Al-Albānī verifies that this report has an authentic *isnād* (chain of narrators) (*al-Āyāt ul-Bayyināt* p. 30 of the introduction).

This is also the understanding of 'Ā'ishah (ﷺ), as is documented in the books of *Sunnah* [1]. It is also the understanding of 'Umar and others among the *ṣaḥābah*.

Those Who Are Worshipped Beside Allāh

Allāh (ﷻ) says:

﴿ذَٰلِكُمُ ٱللَّهُ رَبُّكُمْ لَهُ ٱلْمُلْكُ وَٱلَّذِينَ تَدْعُونَ مِن دُونِهِ مَا يَمْلِكُونَ
مِن قِطْمِيرٍ ۝ إِنْ تَدْعُوهُمْ لَا يَسْمَعُوا۟ دُعَآءَكُمْ وَلَوْ سَمِعُوا۟ مَا ٱسْتَجَابُوا۟
لَكُمْ وَيَوْمَ ٱلْقِيَٰمَةِ يَكْفُرُونَ بِشِرْكِكُمْ وَلَا يُنَبِّئُكَ مِثْلُ خَبِيرٍ ۝﴾

فاطر ١٣-١٤

«Such is Allāh your lord; to Him belongs the dominion. And those, whom you invoke instead of Him, own not even a *qiṭmīr* (date pit's covering membrane). If you call upon them, they do not hear your call; and were they to hear, they could not grant your requests. And on the Day of Resurrection, they will disown your taking them as partners. And none can inform you better than one who is well acquainted with things."» [2]

The disbelievers used to worship a number of people who were righteous and noble during their lifetimes. After their death, Satan inspired their followers to commemorate them with statues. These statues eventually turned into idols that were worshipped instead of Allāh (ﷻ).

The above *āyah* clearly denies that those whom the disbelievers invoked instead of Allāh could hear them. The *āyah* does not refer to the idols themselves, but to the persons whom they were supposed to

1 Check *al-Āyāt ul-Bayyināt* pp. 7, 10, 14, etc.

2 *Fāṭir* 35:13-14.

represent. This clear from the statement, **«On the Day of Resurrection, they will disown your taking them as partners.»** It is not the idols, which are irrational objects, that will be resurrected, but rather the actual people that they represented. There are many *āyāt* in the *Qur'ān* indicating that when Allāh resurrects the people, those who had been worshiped will turn against those who had worshiped them. However, there is nothing to indicate that the irrational objects will be resurrected as well.

Therefore, this *āyah* indicates that the righteous people, as well as those who are of lesser virtue, cannot hear after their death.

The Ditch of Badr

The Combined Report

Ibn ʿUmar, Abū Ṭalḥah, and Anas (ﷺ) reported that, after the battle of Badr, the Prophet (ﷺ) commanded his followers to cast twenty four of the most disdainful among the dead of the Quraysh into a very filthy ditch in Badr. Then, as was his practice after victory, he spent three nights in the neighborhood of the battleground. On the third day, he had his animal prepared for departure, and then went and stood with his companions at the verge of the ditch. He called out the dead men with their names and the names of their parent saying:

> **‹O such and such, son of such and such! O such and such, son of such and such! ... Don't you wish that you had obeyed Allāh and His Messenger? Indeed, we have found our Lord's promises to us true; have you found you Lord's promises true?›**

Whereupon ʿUmar (ﷺ) (and others) exclaimed, "Are you addressing them after having been dead for three nights, and when these bodies have no souls in them? Can they hear? Allāh (ﷻ) says:

﴿إِنَّكَ لَا تُسْمِعُ ٱلْمَوْتَىٰ﴾

«Verily, you cannot make the dead hear you.»"

He (ﷺ) replied:

> ‹By Him in whose hand is Muḥammad's soul, They
> can hear me NOW; and you cannot hear what I am
> saying better than they can! But they cannot
> respond.› [1]

When this incident was mentioned to 'Ā'ishah (﵂), she said, "The
Prophet (ﷺ) only meant that they now realized that what he told them
was the truth." Then she recited the *āyah*:

﴿إِنَّكَ لَا تُسْمِعُ ٱلْمَوْتَىٰ وَلَا تُسْمِعُ ٱلصُّمَّ ٱلدُّعَآءَ إِذَا وَلَّوْاْ مُدْبِرِينَ ۝﴾

> «So, verily you cannot make the dead hear you, nor
> can you make the deaf hear the call while they turn
> their backs to you.» [2]

Commenting on the above *ḥadīth*, Qatādah (﵂) said:

> "Allāh (ﷻ) gave them life in order to hear the
> Prophet's (ﷺ) words, as a reproach and scorn, and to
> make them feel the remorse and regret for what they
> did." [3]

Ibn 'Aṭiyyah [4] said:

> "It appears that the incident of Badr constitutes a
> miracle for Muhammad (ﷺ), whereupon Allāh (ﷻ)

---

1   This is a combined report from three authentic *ḥadīth*s recorded by al-Bukhārī,
    Muslim, and Aḥmad.
2   This is recorded by al-Bukhārī, Aḥmad, and others.
3   Recorded by al-Bukhārī and Muslim.
4   He is a knowledgeable scholar of *Ḥadīth* and *Islām*ic legislation from Grenada, al-
    Andalus (Spain). He has a well-known book of *tafsīr* called "*Al-Muḥarrar ul-Wajīz
    fī Tafsīr il-Kitāb il-'Azīz.* He died on 542 H.

give them back the perception to be able to hear him. Had Allāh's Messenger (ﷺ) not told us of this, we would have interpreted his addressing them to carry the meaning of reproach for the living disbelievers, as well as a reassurance for the hearts of the believers." [1]

Ibn Ḥajar al-ʿAsqalānī (رحمه الله) said:

"Ibn ut-Tīn said, 'There is no conflict between of Ibn ʿUmar's ḥadīth (of the Ditch) and the āyah. There is no doubt that the dead cannot hear. But Allāh may enable that which does not normally hear to hear ...'" [2]

THE PROPHET'S APPROVAL

It is important to point out that the Prophet (ﷺ) approved of the understanding of ʿUmar and others among the ṣaḥābah that the dead cannot hear. We should assume that these companions have previously gained this understanding from the Prophet (ﷺ) – otherwise, they would not have hastened to object to his action of addressing the dead. And even if we assume that they were hasty in objecting without knowledge, it would then be the Prophet's (ﷺ) obligation to clarify to them their misconception. However, he did not do any of that, but only indicated that those specific dead people were able to hear him at that specific time. Thus it is obvious that he (ﷺ) approved of their general understanding in regard to this issue.

And ʿĀʾishah's (رضي الله عنها) above statement (p. 73) shows that she had a similar understanding to that of ʿUmar and the other companions.

WRONG CONCLUSION

This is important to emphasize, especially when we realize that some scholars misinterpret this incident of the Ditch. They use the Prophet's (ﷺ) statement, ‹You cannot hear me better than they can,› as a proof that the dead always hear what goes on around them.

---

1   Al-Qurṭubī's Tafsīr 13:232.
2   Fatḥ ul-Bārī 3:182.

They often neglect the fact that he (ﷺ) has approved of their understanding and did not object to it. Thus, they turn the exceptional case, which was a miracle granted to the Prophet (ﷺ) in that situation, into a general case conflicting with the clear texts of the *Qur'ān*!

A *SUNNAH* OF THE PROPHETS

It is interesting to indicate that addressing the disbeliever after they have been destroyed by Allāh (ﷻ) is an old practice of the prophets. For instance, Allāh (ﷻ) says in regard to the people of Ṣāliḥ:

﴿فَأَخَذَتْهُمُ ٱلرَّجْفَةُ فَأَصْبَحُوا۟ فِي دَارِهِمْ جَـٰثِمِينَ ۝ فَتَوَلَّىٰ عَنْهُمْ وَقَالَ يَـٰقَوْمِ لَقَدْ أَبْلَغْتُكُمْ رِسَالَةَ رَبِّي وَنَصَحْتُ لَكُمْ وَلَـٰكِن لَّا تُحِبُّونَ ٱلنَّـٰصِحِينَ۝﴾ الأعراف ٧٨-٧٩

«So the earthquake seized them, and they became in their homes (corpses) fallen prone. He (Ṣāliḥ) turned away from them and said, "O my people! I have certainly conveyed to you the message of my Lord and advised you; but you do not like advisers.» [1]

Ibn Kathīr commented on this by saying:

> "This is a rebuke from Ṣāliḥ (ﷺ) to his people after Allāh had destroyed them because of their disobeying him, rebelling against Allāh, rejecting the truth, and turning away from the guidance. Ṣāliḥ said this to them, after their destruction, rebuking and reprimanding them; and they heard him, as has been reported in the two *Ṣaḥīḥ*s (Al-Bukhārī and Muslim) … "

He then cited the *ḥadīth* of the Ditch. Note that the *Qur'ān*ic text does not express that they heard Ṣāliḥ. But Ibn Kathīr assumed this based on the similar situation of the Ditch.

1 *Al-A'rāf* 7:78-79.

The Roaming Angels

Ibn Mas'ūd (ﷺ) reported that the Prophet (ﷺ):

> **‹Allāh has angels that roam over the earth, delivering to me the *salām* from my *Ummah*.›** [1]

Similar *ḥadīths* have been cited earlier (p. 50). They clearly indicate that the Prophet (ﷺ) cannot independently hear the *salām* of the Mulsims, but needs angels to deliver it to him. This implies that he cannot hear other things as well. Also, the text of this *ḥadīth* is general and makes no distinction based on distance.

Thus, if Allāh's Messenger (ﷺ) cannot hear after his death what goes on the earth, this should apply more appropriately to those who are lesser than him.

Hearing the Footsteps of His Companions

An important evidence used by those who believe that the dead hear what goes on the earth is the Prophet's (ﷺ) description in the long *ḥadīth* of al-Barā' Bin 'Āzib (fully cited in Chapter 2):

> **‹He hears the thumping of his companions' shoes as they walk away from his grave.›**

However, this clearly applies to the time when the dead person is put into his grave and the angels come to question him. It cannot be generalized to other cases. This is the only way to reconcile between the general meaning of the above *āyah* (as understood by 'Umar, 'Ā'ishah, and other companions) and this *ḥadīth*.

1 Recorded by Abū Dāwūd and others. Verified to be authentic by al-Albānī (*al-Āyāt ul-Bayyināt* p. 43).

CHAPTER 11

THINGS THAT BENEFIT THE DEAD

Introduction

This worldly life is a life of tests and trials. A person's performance in it determines his fate in the hereafter. His actions are recorded, and are the basis for his judgement in the next life.

Allāh (ﷻ) informs us that a disbeliever's punishment is a result of his actions:

﴿ذَٰلِكَ بِمَا قَدَّمَتْ أَيْدِيكُمْ وَأَنَّ ٱللَّهَ لَيْسَ بِظَلَّامٍ لِّلْعَبِيدِ ۝﴾

آل عمران ١٨٢

«This (punishment) is because of that which your hands have previously done. Certainly, Allāh is never unjust to His slaves.» [1]

Allāh (ﷻ) also informs us that a believer's rewards result from his actions:

﴿وَتِلْكَ ٱلْجَنَّةُ ٱلَّتِي أُورِثْتُمُوهَا بِمَا كُنتُمْ تَعْمَلُونَ ۝﴾ الزخرف ٧٢

«This is *Jannah* which you have been made to inherit because of the deeds that you used to do.» [2]

Thus, the deeds that a person can do in this life to benefit him on the Day of judgement end by his death. Allāh (ﷻ) says:

﴿وَلَيْسَتِ ٱلتَّوْبَةُ لِلَّذِينَ يَعْمَلُونَ ٱلسَّيِّئَاتِ حَتَّىٰٓ إِذَا حَضَرَ أَحَدَهُمُ

1 *Āl 'Imrān* 3:182, *al-Anfāl* 8:51, and *al-Ḥajj* 22:10.

2 *Az-Zukhruf* 43:72.

ٱلۡمَوۡتُ قَالَ إِنِّي تُبۡتُ ٱلۡـَٰٔنَ وَلاَ ٱلَّذِينَ يَمُوتُونَ وَهُمۡ كُفَّارٌ ۩﴾

النساء ١٨

«And of no effect is the repentance of those who continue to do evil deeds until death faces one of them and he says, "Now I repent;" nor of those who die while they are disbelievers.» [1]

And Ibn 'Umar (ﷺ) reported that Allāh's Messenger (ﷺ) said:

‹Allāh accepts a person's repentance as long as he does not reach the gurgling stage (when his soul departs).› [2]

Therefore, one cannot expect any changes in his records after departing from this world.

Furthermore, one cannot expect other people to do for him, after his death, good deeds that will benefit him in the hereafter. Allāh (ﷻ) says:

﴿وَأَن لَّيۡسَ لِلۡإِنسَـٰنِ إِلاَّ مَا سَعَىٰ ۩﴾ النجم ٣٩

«And that the human being can have nothing but what he has earned (good or bad).» [3]

Commenting on this *āyah*, Ibn Kathīr (رحمه الله) said:

"Imām ash-Shāfi'ī concluded from this *āyah* that reciting *Qur'ān* does not benefit the dead, because it is not from their doing and earning. For this reason, Allāh's Messenger (ﷺ) did not recommend it to his *Ummah*, encourage them to do it, or guide them to it with a text or a hint. Nor was such a thing reported from any of the *ṣaḥābah* (رضي الله عنهم). Had this been any good,

---

1   *An-Nisā'* 4:18.
2   Recorded by Aḥmad, at-Tirmithī, and others. Verified to be authentic by al-Albānī.
3   *An-Najm* 53:39.

> they would have preceded us in doing it. Matters of worship must be limited to the texts, and are not liable to modifications based on analogies and opinions." [1]

It is in general true that one cannot benefit from other people's deeds after his death. But this has important exceptions detailed in this chapter.

List of Beneficial Acts

The following list summarizes the beneficial acts, covered in this chapter, that benefit a person after his death.

#	Beneficial Act
1	*Janāzah* prayer for the deceased
2	Deeds of renewed benefit
3	Charitable deeds from a child
4	Fulfilling the deceased's vows
5	Payment of the deceased's debts
6	Supplications of the Muslims
7	Guarding in Allāh's way
8	Reviving the *Sunnah*

Janāzah Prayer

When the Muslims pray *janāzah* for their deceased brother, they are granted intercession for him. The more the number of Muslims who join in the prayer, the more beneficial it is for the deceased.

1 *Tafsīr ul-Qur'ān il-'Aẓīm.*

This means that Allāh takes their testimony and supplication regarding the deceased's apparent actions as a sufficient reason for forgiveness. Since those Muslims who associated with him did not find any major problem to prevent them from supplicating for him, Allāh the most generous accepts that and agrees to forgive many of his hidden sins that they did not know. Anas and 'Ā'ishah (🌸) reported that Allāh's Messenger (🌸) said:

〈Whenever a (Muslim) person dies, and a group of Muslims numbering one hundred pray *janāzah* for him, all interceding on his behalf, their intercession is granted (by Allāh), and he is forgiven.〉 [1]

Ibn 'Abbās (🌸) reported that Allāh's Messenger (🌸) said:

〈Whenever a Muslim man dies, and forty men stand for his *janāzah* prayer, all of them not joining anything with Allāh in worship, Allāh grants them intercession for him.〉 [2]

Maymūnah (🌸) reported that Allāh's Messenger (🌸) said:

〈Whenever a (Muslim) person dies, and a group of (Muslim) people pray *janāzah* for him, they are granted intercession for him.〉 [3]

Mālik Bin Hubayrah (🌸) reported that Allāh's Messenger (🌸) said:

〈Whenever a Muslim dies, and three lines of Muslims pray *janāzah* for him, he is granted forgiveness.〉 [4]

---

1   Muslim and others

2   Muslim and others

3   Recorded by an-Nasā'ī; verified to be *hasan* by al-Albānī (*Sahīh ul-Jāmi'* no. 5787).

4   Recorded by Ahmad, Abū Dāwūd, and others. Verified to be *hasan* by al-Hāfiz and others; however, al-Albānī disagrees with this because Muhammad Bin Ishāq, one of the narrators, is known to be a *mudallis* (one who is ambiguous in stating his

Shams ul-Ḥaqq Ābādī said in his commentary on *Sunan Abī Dāwūd*:

> "These *ḥadīths* indicate that it is recommended to gather a large number of people for the *janāzah* prayer. It should be attempted to reach these numbers (mentioned in the *ḥadīths*), because that could lead to success (in the forgiveness of the deceased). This has been restricted by two conditions:
>
> 1) They should attempt to intercede for him, which means that they should be sincere in supplication and in seeking forgiveness for him.
>
> 2) They should all be Muslims, none among them joining partners with Allāh, as in the earlier *ḥadīth* of Ibn ʿAbbās." [1]

Deeds of Renewed Benefit

Any good deed that a Muslim starts during his lifetime, and that is of renewed benefit and ongoing use for the Muslims, will continue to benefit him and augment his record of good deeds, even after his departure – as long as its benefits continue to reach others. Allāh (ﷻ) says:

﴿وَنَكْتُبُ مَا قَدَّمُوا۟ وَءَاثَـٰرَهُمْ﴾ يس ١٢

> **«We record that (deeds) which they have put forward, and their traces (that which they have left behind).»** [2]

sources), and did not declare direct hearing of this report (*Aḥkām ul-Janāʾiz* 128). Yet, the Prophet's (ﷺ) practice of forming three lines for *janāzah* prayer provides a further supporting evidence for this *ḥadīth*.

1 ʿ*Awn ul-Maʿbūd* 8:452.

2 *Yā-Sīn* 36:12.

Abū Hurayrah (ﷺ) reported that Allāh's Messenger (ﷺ) said:

> **‹When a human being dies, all of his deeds are terminated except for three types: an ongoing *ṣadaqah*, a knowledge (of *Islām*) from which others benefit, and a righteous child who makes *Du'ā'* for him.›** [1]

Abū Qatādah (ﷺ) reported that Allāh's Messenger (ﷺ) said:

> **‹The best that a man can leave behind after his death are three things: a righteous child who makes *Du'ā'* for him, an ongoing *ṣadaqah* whose rewards continue to reach him, and a knowledge that continues to be implemented after him.›** [2]

Abū Qatādah (ﷺ) also reported that Allāh's Messenger (ﷺ) said:

> **‹Among the good deeds that continue to benefit a believer after death are: a knowledge that he taught and disseminated, a righteous child who lived after him, a *Qur'ān* book that he left as inheritance, a *masjid* (mosque) that he built, a house that he built for the wayfarers, a stream that he ran, or a charity that he gave from his wealth during his healthy lifetime so that it would reach him (in rewards) after death.›** [3]

Commenting on this, al-Mun<u>th</u>irī (ﷺ) said:

> "Some scholars say that the deeds of a human being end with his death. However, since he had caused these

1 Muslim and others.

2 Recorded by Ibn Mājah and others. Verified to be authentic by al-Mun<u>th</u>irī and al-Albānī.

3 Recorded by Ibn Mājah and others. Verified to be *ḥasan* by al-Mun<u>th</u>irī and al-Albānī.

> things (which are mentioned in the above *ḥadīth*s), such as the earning of a child, disseminating the knowledge among those who take it from him, compiling a book that remains after him, or establishing a *ṣadaqah*, the rewards of these things continue to reach him as long as they continue to exist." [1]

The reason that one continues to receive rewards for these deeds, even though they are done by other people, is that he had initiated them during his life or contributed to them to a certain degree, whether little or large. Since Allāh does not neglect an atom's weight of deeds, He records these contribution for a person even after his death. Abū al-Wafā' Bin 'Aqīl said:

> "The best explanation for this in my view is that a human being, by his efforts and good conduct, had earned friends, produced children, married spouses, done good, and was amiable to the people. Because of this, they invoke mercy for him and do good on his behalf. All of this is then a result of his own earning." [2]

And Rashīd Riḍā (ﷺ) said:

> "Among the deeds that benefit a person, even though they are done by others, are those that count like his own because he caused them, such as his children's supplication for him, or their performing *ḥajj*, giving *ṣadaqah*, or fasting on his behalf – all of which having been established with authentic *ḥadīth*s." [3]

1 *'Awn ul-Ma'būd* 8:86.

2 Cited in *ar-Rūḥ* by Ibn ul-Qayyim p. 171.

3 *Tafsīr ul-Manār* 8:247.

Charitable Deeds from a Child

ONE'S CHILD IS FROM HIS EARNING

The above *ḥadīth*s indicate that a righteous child benefits his deceased parents with *du'ā'*. It is further demonstrated here that he can benefit them by spending *ṣadaqah*, as well as doing other charitable deeds, on their behalf.

'Ā'ishah (⁂) reported that Allāh's Messenger (⁂) said:

> ‹Indeed, the best that one eats is that which he earns. And his child is from his earning.› [1]

The reason for this is that a parent benefits himself by rearing his child according to the teachings of *Islām*, and exerting a consistent effort to raise him as a righteous person. As the child grows into adulthood and does righteous deeds, his parents deserve a merit in that they helped him accomplish that; and his good actions are therefore, at least in part, from his parents' earning.

ṢADAQAH FROM A CHILD

'Ā'ishah (⁂) reported that a man asked Allāh's Messenger (⁂), "My mother had a sudden death, and did not have chance to bequeath anything. Had she been able to do, I think that she would have given *ṣadaqah*. Would she or I get any rewards if I give *ṣadaqah* on her behalf?" He (⁂) replied, ‹Yes! So give *ṣadaqah* on her behalf.› [2]

Ibn 'Abbās (⁂) reported that Sa'd Bin 'Ubādah's mother died during his absence on a trip. He came to the Prophet (⁂) and asked him, "O Allāh's Messenger! My mother has passed away during my absence. Would it be of benefit to her if I give *ṣadaqah* on her behalf?" He (⁂) replied, ‹Yes!› He said, "Be my witness then that I give my fruitful garden as *ṣadaqah* on her behalf." [3]

---

1 Recorded by Aḥmad, Abū Dāwūd, and others. Verified to be authentic by al-Albānī (*Aḥkām ul-Janā'iz* 217).

2 Al-Bukhārī, Muslim, and others.

3 Al-Bukhārī, Aḥmad, and others.

Abū Hurayrah (⬥) reported that a man asked the Prophet (⬥), "My father has died, leaving behind a wealth; but he did not bequeath anything. Would it help him if I give *sadaqah* on his behalf?" He (⬥) replied, ‹Yes!› [1]

'Abdullāh Bin 'Amr (⬥) reported that al-'Āṣ Bin Wā'il as-Sahmī (his grandfather) bequeathed that one hundred slaves be freed on his behalf. His son Hishām freed fifty; and 'Amr wanted to free the other fifty, but decided to ask Allāh's Messenger (⬥) first. He came to the Prophet (⬥) and said, "O Allāh's Messenger (⬥)! My father has bequeathed that one hundred slaves be freed on his behalf. Hishām has freed fifty, and fifty are left. Should I free them for him?" He replied:

‹Had he been a Muslim, your freeing slaves, giving *sadaqah*, or performing *hajj* on his behalf would all have reached (in rewards) and benefited him.› [2]

Commenting on these *hadīth*s, ash-Shawkānī said:

"This indicates that the rewards for a *sadaqah* from a child reach the parents after their death – even if they had not bequeathed it. These *hadīth*s restrict the general meaning of Allāh's (⬥) saying:

﴾وَأَن لَّيْسَ لِلْإِنسَـٰنِ إِلَّا مَا سَعَىٰ ۝﴿ النجم ٣٩

«And that the human being can have nothing but what he has earned.» [3]

But there is no indication in these *hadīth*s that the *sadaqah*, except from one's own child, helps. Since it is established that a person's child is his own earning, it is not possible to claim that the meaning (of these *hadīth*s) needs to be restricted.

1   Muslim, Aḥmad, and others.
2   Recorded by Aḥmad, Abū Dāwūd, and al-Bayhaqī. Verified to be *hasan* by al-Albānī (*Aḥkām ul-Janā'iz* 218).
3   *An-Najm* 53:39.

> As for the *ṣadaqah* from other than one's child, it is apparent from general *Qur'ān*ic texts that it does not help the deceased. This should then be maintained unless an additional evidence can be brought to restrict it." [1]

Charitable Deeds from a Non-child

Some scholars, such as an-Nawawī, hold the opinion that all charitable deeds on behalf of a deceased person benefit him, whether done by his children or other people. This is refuted by ash-Shawkānī's above strong argument. Similarly, al-Albānī says in this regard:

> "Some scholars have treated a non-child as a child (in this matter). This analogy is invalid for various reasons:
>
> 1. It conflicts with general *Qur'ān*ic texts that make a person's good deeds a condition for entering *Jannah.* There is no doubt that a parent benefits himself by raising his child and nurturing him. Thus, unlike other people, he deserves a reward for this.
>
> 2. The difference between the two cases inhibits such an analogy. As in 'Ā'ishah's *ḥadīth,* Allāh has made a child part of his parents' earnings – but not of other people's earnings. Al-'Izz Bin 'Abd us-Salām said:
>
>   'If one does an act of obedience and dedicates its reward to a living or dead person, the reward will not reach that person. And if he starts an act of worship intending it on behalf of a dead person, it would not be as intended – except for

1 *Nayl ul-Awṭār* 4:97.

things excluded in *Islām* such as *ṣadaqah*, fasting, and *ḥajj*.' [1]

3. Had this analogy been possible, it would have implied that it is recommended to dedicate rewards to the dead. In such a case, the *Salaf* would have done this, because they surely used to have more concern than us about doing good. But they did not do it. Ibn Taymiyyah said:

   'It was not the practice of the *Salaf*, when they performed a voluntary prayer, fasting, *ḥajj*, or *Qur'ān*ic recitation, to dedicate the rewards of that to the dead Muslims. Thus, one should not abandon the way of the *Salaf*, because it is better and more complete.' [2] " [3]

Claims for *Ijmā'*

It should be noted that there are claims for *ijmā'* (consensus) that a dead person benefits from the good deeds, including *Qur'ān*ic recitation, done on his behalf by other people [4]. Whereas these claims have been demonstrated to be invalid in the above discussion, they further fall under the following two consideration:

1 *Al-Fatāwā* 24:2.

2 *Al-Ikhtiyārāt ul-'Ilmiyyah* 54. Note that Ibn Taymiyyah has another opinion contradicting this one, which was advocated by his student Ibn ul-Qayyim in *ar-Rūḥ*. That opinion conflicts with Ibn Taymiyyah's known position of rejecting *qiyās* (analogy) in matters of worship; and it was refuted in a strong and sound manner by Muḥammad Rashīd Riḍā in *Tafsīr ul-Manār* 8:254-270. Many people of *bid'ah* have used this second opinion of Ibn Taymiyyah as an evidence against the followers of *Sunnah*. By doing this, they have neglected a very important fact, which is that the people of *Sunnah* do not imitate any one specific man without evidence; and they do not blindly imitate any particular scholar, regardless of how much love they hold for him (*Aḥkām ul-Janā'iz* 221-222).

3 Summarized from *Aḥkām ul-Janā'iz* 220-222.

4 Such as an-Nawawī, Ibn Qudāmah (in *al-Mughnī* 2:569), and others.

"1. It has been demonstrated by staunch scholars, such as Ibn Ḥazm (in *Uṣūl ul-Aḥkām*), ash-Shawkānī (in *Irshād ul-Fuḥūl*), and ʿAbd ul-Wahhāb Khallāf (in *Uṣūl ul-Fiqh*), that it is not possible to justify *ijmāʿ* for other than the most obvious matters in *Islām*. Imām Aḥmad has indicated this in his famous refutation against those who claim *ijmāʿ*.

2. I have investigated many of the cases for which there have been claims of *ijmāʿ*, and found that there is an obvious difference of opinion concerning them. I even found (in some cases) that the opinion of the majority of scholars is contrary to the claimed *ijmāʿ*!" [1]

A Dangerous Belief

The danger of holding a wrong belief in regard to this issue has been clarified and emphasized by al-Albānī:

> "We do not doubt this wrong belief's evil effects upon one who adopts it. He would rely upon others for acquiring rewards and high ranks (in the hereafter), because he knows that the Muslims dedicate hundreds of good deeds everyday to all of the living and dead Muslims, and he is one of them; that would then relieve him from having to work hard when others are striving on his behalf! …
>
> A more dangerous saying is that it is permissible to perform *ḥajj* on behalf of others, even if there is no valid excuse preventing them from performing it by themselves. This causes many of the wealthy people to drop *ḥajj* or other obligations, giving themselves the excuse, 'They will perform *ḥajj* on my behalf after my death!' …

1 Al-Albānī in *Aḥkām ul-Janāʾiz* 219.

There are many other similar opinions that clearly have evil effects on the (Muslim) societies. It is imperative for the scholars who wish to reform (the societies) to reject such opinions, because they conflict with the texts, as well as the spirit of the *Sharī'ah*. ...

As for the person who rejects the opinions described above, it is inconceivable that he would ever rely on other people in doing deeds and acquiring rewards. He realizes that only his own deeds can save him, and he is rewarded in accordance with what he himself earns. It is then incumbent that he strives to the utmost to leave behind him good traces which will result in good rewards for him even in the loneliness of his grave – instead of those imaginary good deeds." [1]

Fulfilling the Deceased's Vows

Fasting the Vowed Days

'Ā'ishah (رضي الله عنها) reported that Allāh's Messenger (ﷺ) said:

> **‹Whoever dies while he has a fasting to fulfill (as a vow), his *walī* [2] should fast for him.›** [3]

Ibn 'Abbās (رضي الله عنهما) reported that a woman was travelling in the sea, and she vowed that if Allāh saved her she would fast for one month. Allāh saved her, but she died before fulfilling her vow. Her daughter came to the Prophet (ﷺ) and mentioned this to him. He asked, **‹Had she owed money as debt, wouldn't you have paid it on her behalf?›** She replied, "Yes." He said:

1 *Aḥkām ul-Janā'iz* 222-223.

2 Next of kin or guardian.

3 Al-Bukhārī, Muslim, and others.

‹Allāh's debt is more worthy of being fulfilled. So fulfill (the vow) for your mother.› [1]

Sa'd Bin 'Ubādah reported that he told Allāh's Messenger (ﷺ), "My mother has died; and she had an unfulfilled vow." He instructed him:

‹Fulfill it for her.› [2]

These *ḥadīth*s clearly indicate that it is recommended for a deceased's *walī* to fulfill his vows for fasting.

Fasting the Missed Days of *Ramaḍān*

Some scholars recommended, in addition to this, fasting the days of *Ramaḍān* that the deceased had missed. However, the correct position in this regard is expressed by Imām Aḥmad (رحمه الله):

"One may not fast for a dead person except in the case of a vow." [3]

This position is confirmed by the understanding of two of the *ṣaḥābah*: 'Ā'ishah (رضي الله عنها) and Ibn 'Abbās (رضي الله عنه).

'Amrah reported that her mother died without making up her missed days of *Ramaḍān*. She asked 'Ā'ishah (رضي الله عنها), "Should I make that up on her behalf?" She replied:

"No! Rather, give *ṣadaqah* to the needy in the amount of a half *ṣā'* [4] (of grains or food) for every missed day." [5]

1 Al-Bukhārī, Muslim, and others.

2 Al-Bukhārī, Muslim, and others.

3 *Al-Masā'il* 96 by Abū Dāwūd.

4 A *ṣā'* is a measure approximately equal to four scoops, with the hands cupped together, of an average man.

5 Recorded by aṭ-Ṭaḥāwī and Ibn Ḥazm. Verified to be authentic by al-Albānī (*Aḥkām ul-Janā'iz* 215).

Saʿīd Bin Jubayr (رضي الله عنه) reported that Ibn ʿAbbās (رضي الله عنهما) said:

"If a man gets sick in *Ramaḍān* and then dies without fasting, food should be given on his behalf – without a need to make up for the fasting. But if he had made a vow (to fast), his *walī* should fast for him." [1]

Commenting on this, al-Albānī says:

"This understanding is adopted by the Mother of the Believers, as well as Ibn ʿAbbās, the great scholar of the *Ummah*, and is further held by the *Imām* of *Sunnah*, Aḥmad Bin Ḥanbal. It is the most moderate and appropriate opinion in this regard; and it fulfills all of the relevant *ḥadīth*s, without rejecting any of them, especially the first, which the Mother of the Believers (رضي الله عنها) did not find applicable to the fasting of *Ramaḍān*. She is the reporter of the *ḥadīth*, and it is established that a narrator of a *ḥadīth* is more knowledgeable about the meaning of what he reports, especially when his understanding agrees with the rules and foundations of the *Sharīʿah* [2], as is the case here." [3]

And Ibn ul-Qayyim (رحمه الله) comments on ʿĀʾishah's above *ḥadīth* by saying:

"One group (of scholars) generalizes this, and says that both the vowed and missed obligatory fasting should be made up for the deceased. Another group rejects this and says that no fasting may be made up for him. A third group is more specific in saying that only the vowed fasting, but not the obligatory fasting, should be

---

1   Recorded by Abū Dāwūd and Ibn Ḥazm. Verified to be authentic by al-Albānī (*Aḥkām ul-Janāʾiz* 215).
2   *Sharīʿah* or *Sharʿ*: Islāmic law and instructions.
3   *Aḥkām ul-Janāʾiz* 215-216.

fasted on his behalf. This is the opinion of Ibn 'Abbās and his followers, and is the correct opinion.

Just as it is not possible for one to pray on behalf of another, or embrace *Islām* on his behalf, the same is true about fasting. As for a vow, it represents a committed obligation similar to a debt. Thus, the *walī*'s execution is acceptable, as in the case of the debt. This is the pure understanding (of this issue).

By the same token, it is not possible to perform *hajj* (pilgrimage) or *zakāh* (obligatory charity) on behalf of the deceased unless he had an acceptable excuse in delaying that. This is similar to a *walī*'s feeding the needy on behalf of the one who broke his fast in *Ramadān* with a valid excuse. But as for the one who neglected his obligations without a valid excuse, it would not help him that others perform his neglected obligations, because he was the one required to perform them as a test for him – not the *walī*. Thus, no one may repent on behalf of someone else, nor accept *Islām*, nor perform the prayers or other obligations that he neglected until death." [1]

Payment of the Deceased's Debts

The deceased's debts should be paid off immediately after his death. The *walī* should use whatever wealth the deceased had left behind. If that is exhausted, he should seek the help of relatives and friends of the deceased who are capable of helping in paying off the rest of the debt. There is a number of *hadīths* in this regard that we have included in Part 3 of this series. We mention one of them here for reference.

Saʿd Bin al-Aṭwal (⬥) reported that his brother died, leaving behind three hundred *dirhams* and children. He wanted to spend the money on his brother's children, but the Prophet (⬥) told him:

1 *Iʿlām ul-Muwaqqiʿīn* 3:554.

‹Your brother is a captive because of his debt. Go pay it off for him.› [1]

The Muslims' Supplications

A Muslim's *du'ā'* for a dead Muslim tremendously benefits both of them. When it is done correctly, truthfully, and sincerely, it reflects a high level of brotherhood and concern; and it eliminates the factor of showoff which can potentially destroy the good deeds. Allāh (ﷻ) says:

﴿وَٱلَّذِينَ جَآءُو مِنۢ بَعْدِهِمْ يَقُولُونَ رَبَّنَا ٱغْفِرْ لَنَا
وَلِإِخْوَٰنِنَا ٱلَّذِينَ سَبَقُونَا بِٱلْإِيمَٰنِ﴾ الحشر ١٠

«And those who came (into the faith) after them say: "Our Lord! Forgive us and our brothers who preceded us in *Īmān*." » [2]

'Ubādah (ﷺ) reported that Allāh's Messenger (ﷺ) said:

‹Whoever seeks forgiveness for the believing men and women, Allāh records for him a good deed for every believing man and woman.› [3]

Abū ad-Dardā' (ﷺ) reported that Allāh's Messenger (ﷺ) said:

‹A Muslim's supplication for his brother in his absence is acceptable. An angel is appointed to stand by his head; every time he invokes something good

1 Recorded by Aḥmad, Ibn Mājah, and al-Bayhaqī. Verified to be authentic by al-Albānī (*Aḥkām ul-Janā'iz* 26).

2 *Al-Ḥashr* 59:10.

3 Recorded by Aṭ-Ṭabarānī in *al-Kabīr*; verified to be *ḥasan* by al-Albānī (*Ṣaḥīḥ ul-Jāmi'* no. 6026).

for his brother, the appointed angels says, "*Āmīn*[1]; and the same be given to you."›[2]

Guarding in Allāh's Way

As has been previously demonstrated (p. 66) Standing guard in the way of Allāh (ﷻ) benefits a person after his death. Fuḍālah Bin ʿUbayd and ʿUqbah Bin ʿĀmir (ﷺ) reported that Allāh's Messenger (ﷺ) said:

‹The deeds of a dead person are sealed (at the time of death), except for the one who stands guard in the way of Allāh: his (good) deeds continue to increase until the Day of Resurrection, and he is protected from the trial of the grave.›[3]

Reviving the *Sunnah*

Calling to a forgotten *Sunnah* or fighting an established *bidʿah* are among the most important charitable deeds that a person can do during his lifetime. They help revive Allāh's *Dīn* and enable other people to follow it clean and pure, as it was revealed to Muḥammad (ﷺ).

Jarīr Bin ʿAbdillāh (ﷺ) reported that they (the companions) were with Allāh's Messenger (ﷺ) in the middle of the day when a group of people arrived (from outside al-Madīnah) to see him. They were barefoot, (almost) naked, wearing only woolen lined cloth pieces or cloaks, armed with swords, wearing no *izārs*[4] or anything else beside that. Most or all of them were from (the tribe of) Muḍar. The face of Allāh's Messenger (ﷺ) changed (reflecting sadness) when he noticed their extreme poverty. He went in (to his house), then came out. He commanded Bilāl to give *athān* (prayer announcement), prayed *ẓuhr*

1 This means, "O my Lord! Answer me!"

2 Muslim and others.

3 Recorded by Aḥmad, Abū Dāwūd, at-Tirmithī, and others; verified to be authentic by al-Albānī (*Ṣaḥīḥ ul-Jāmiʿ* no. 4562).

4 *Izār*: a plain piece of clothing tied around the lower section of the body.

(midday prayer), then mounted a small *minbar* (steps). He gave a *khutbah* (speech) in which he praised and thanked Allāh, and then said:

‹After this, (I say that) Allāh has revealed in His book:

﴿يَا أَيُّهَا ٱلنَّاسُ ٱتَّقُوا رَبَّكُمُ ٱلَّذِي خَلَقَكُمْ مِنْ نَفْسٍ وَاحِدَةٍ وَخَلَقَ مِنْهَا زَوْجَهَا وَبَثَّ مِنْهُمَا رِجَالاً كَثِيرًا وَنِسَآءً ۚ وَٱتَّقُواْ ٱللَّهَ ٱلَّذِي تَسَآءَلُونَ بِهِ وَٱلْأَرْحَامَ ۚ إِنَّ ٱللَّهَ كَانَ عَلَيْكُمْ رَقِيبًا۝﴾ النساء ١

«O people! Revere your Lord who has created you from one soul, and created from it its mate, and from these two spread forth multitudes of men and women; and fear Allāh through whom you demand [your mutual rights], and [revere the ties of] the wombs. Indeed, Allāh is ever-watchful over you.» [1]

And He (ﷻ) says:

﴿يَـٰأَيُّهَا ٱلَّذِينَ ءَامَنُواْ ٱتَّقُواْ ٱللَّهَ وَلْتَنظُرْ نَفْسٌ مَّا قَدَّمَتْ لِغَدٍ وَٱتَّقُواْ ٱللَّهَ ۚ إِنَّ ٱللَّهَ خَبِيرٌ بِمَا تَعْمَلُونَ۝ وَلَا تَكُونُواْ كَٱلَّذِينَ نَسُواْ ٱللَّهَ فَأَنسَـٰهُمْ أَنفُسَهُمْ ۚ أُوْلَـٰئِكَ هُمُ ٱلْفَـٰسِقُونَ ۝ لَا يَسْتَوِي أَصْحَـٰبُ ٱلنَّارِ وَأَصْحَـٰبُ ٱلْجَنَّةِ ۚ أَصْحَـٰبُ ٱلْجَنَّةِ هُمُ ٱلْفَآئِزُونَ ۝﴾ الحشر ١٨–٢٠

«O you who believe! Revere Allāh, and let every person look to what he has sent forth for the morrow; and revere Allāh. Allāh is well Aware of what you do! And be not like those who forgot (disobeyed) Allāh, and He caused them to forget themselves. Those are the disobedient. Not equal are

1 *An-Nisā'* 4:1.

the dwellers of the Fire and the dwellers of *Jannah*. It is the dwellers of *Jannah* that will be successful.» [1]

Spend (in Allāh's way) before you are prevented from spending. Let a man spend of his *dīnārs*, *dirhams*, clothes, measure of wheat, barley, or dates.›

Until he (ﷺ) said:

‹Do not belittle any amount of *ṣadaqah* (charity). Safeguard yourselves from the Fire, even with half a date.›

Observing the people's slow response, the Prophet's (ﷺ) face showed signs of anger. But then, one man from the *Anṣār* came with a parcel full (of money) of silver and gold, which he could hardly hold in his palm. He handed it to Allāh's Messenger (ﷺ), while he was still on the *minbar*, and said, "O Allāh's Messenger! Take this in Allāh's way." He (ﷺ) took it. Abū Bakr (رضي الله عنه) then stood and gave something. Then ʿUmar (رضي الله عنه) gave something. Then the rest of the *Muhājrūn* and *Anṣār* gave. Thus people followed each other in giving charity: This would give a *dīnār*, this a *dirham*, this such, and this such – until there were two piles of food and clothes; and the face of Allāh's Messenger (ﷺ) lighted up with a reddish-golden color. So he said:

‹He who initiates in *Islām* a good way gets his reward for it, as well as rewards similar to those who follow him into it, without reducing any of their rewards. And he who initiates in *Islām* an evil way gets his burden for it, as well as burdens similar to those who follow him into it, without reducing any of their burdens.›

He (ﷺ) then recited:

1 *Al-Ḥashr* 59:18-20.

﴿وَنَكْتُبُ مَا قَدَّمُوا۟ وَءَاثَـٰرَهُمْ وَكُلَّ شَىْءٍ أَحْصَيْنَـٰهُ
فِىٓ إِمَامٍ مُّبِينٍ ۝﴾ يس ١٢

«We record that which they have done, as well as their traces – and We have enumerated everything in a clear book.» [1]

And he divided what was collected among them (the poor people from Muḍar*)*. [2]

Conclusion

From the above discussion, we can conclude that:

1. A person's deeds are sealed by his death. Nothing that takes place after that can affect his records.

2. The exception to the above rule is that anything, good or bad, that takes place after a person's death, which he contributed to its occurrence in any manner during his lifetime, will appear in his records in proportion with his contribution to it.

1 *Yā-Sīn* 36:12.

2 This combined report is taken from Muslim, Aḥmad, and others (*aḥkām ul-Janā'iz* 224-226).

REFERENCES

Aḥkām ul-Janā'izi wa-Bida'uhā (The Regulations of Funerals, and Innovations Thereof), Muḥammad Nāṣir ud-Dīn il-Albānī, Maktabat ul-Ma'ārif, Riyadh, 1993.

Al-Āyāt ul-Bayyināt, Fī 'Adami Samā' il-Amwāt (The Clear Signs Concerning the Inability of the Dead to Hear), Nu'mān Bin Maḥmūd al-Ālūsī and Muḥammad Nāṣir ud-Dīn il-Albānī, 1398 H (1977).

Al-Mawt, 'Iẓātuhu wa-Aḥkāmuh (Death, Its Lessons and Legislations), 'Alī Ḥasan 'Abdulḥamīd al-Ḥalabī.

Al-Qabr, 'Athābuhū wa-Na'īmuh (The Grave, Its Tortures and Pleasures), Ḥusayn al-'Awāyshah.

An-Nadāmat ul-Kubrā (The Great Regret), Muḥammad Shūmān ar-Ramlī, Dār Ibn 'Affān, al-Khubar, Saudi Arabia, 1994.

An-Nathīr uṣ-Ṣārikh Ḥawl al-Mawti wa-Ahl il-Barāzikh (The Outcrying Warner Regarding Death and the People of *al-Barzakh*), Muḥammad Bin 'Abdillāh 'Alī al-Ḥakamī, Dār ul-Majtama', Jeddah, 1995.

'Athāb ul-Qabri wa-Na'īmuh, wa-'Iẓat ul-Mawt (The Tortures and Pleasures of the Grave, and the Lesson of Death), 'Abdullatīf 'Āshūr.

Mā Yanfa' ul-Muslima ba'da Wafātih (That Which Benefits a Muslim after His Death), Ibrāhīm Bin Muḥammad, Maktabat uṣ-Ṣaḥābah, Ṭanṭā, Egypt, 1987.

Sharḥ us-Sunnah (The Explanation of *Sunnah*), Al-Baghawī.